The '90s
Life on the Road

T. J. Wray

ISBN - 978-1-0878-1827-6 (Paperback)
ASIN - B07L2CNBFV - (Digital)

Copyright 2018 T. J. Wray
All rights reserved
First Edition

No part of this publication may be reproduced, distributed, or transmitted in any form or by any means, including photocopying, recording, or any other electronic or mechanical methods without the prior written permission of the publisher
T. J. Wray.

Table of Contents

1. Introduction (Back!) Again
2. Not an Auto Mechanic!
3. On the Road Again
4. Canada 'eh?
5. Just Glad to Be Back on American Soil
6. Go West Young Man
7. Another New Truck
8. Hitchhiking with a CDL
9. HOTDOG
10. As a Child
11. Alligator - Alligator
12. There Ain't No Feelin, Like 18 Wheelin
13. Back Home
14. Just F.Y.I.

Dedication

About the Author

Chapter - One
Introduction

Again, (just as in my other books), I would like to apologize in advance for my broken version of the English language. I'm not politically correct and I don't speak proper English. I'm from Texas and I say Howdy, Y'all and Ain't. Plus, I failed English class in school. I was one of those kids who preferred Math or History. I still do. So please forgive me.

This book is based on facts and is a true story to the very best of my memory. I hope you enjoy reading it as much as I have enjoyed telling these stories and writing them down. This book is the second book in the (My Life) series. If you enjoy it, please share it with someone you love. God bless you and your family.

T.J.

Howdy, my name is T.J. If you read my first book, (Our Teenage Years: Growing up in a small town in the '80s), you will understand exactly where I am coming from. That book was about the 1980s and all my wild teenage experiences. That book was about my best friend Terry and I, Terry recently passed away. After the '80s and our teenage years Terry and I kind of went in two different directions.

We went to different colleges and we both got married and had children. We remained good buddies over the years but were never as close as we had been in our teenage years. We did have some epic fishing trips and wild adventures, but that was in our younger years. Once we started having children, I guess we were forced to be adults and role models for our children, so we grew out of a lot of the wild things we had done as teenagers. Plus, as we got older, we started taking fewer risks and became less adventurous.

This book is the second book I have written about my life's adventures. You will feel as though we are already friends if you read my first book. This book is about the 1990s and much more grown-up and adult experiences. The '90s were both good, and bad, for me. At the beginning of the '90s, I broke my back and went through some very serious rehab after the surgery. Later, in the '90s, I had some wondrous experiences, like watching my daughter Melissa grow up and become a young lady.

I also went on the road for two years and drove a Big Truck across the country. During those two years, I visited some 45 of the 48 states. I went to Canada four times, and Mexico several times and just about everywhere in between. I drove a Big Truck nearly a half of a million miles across America, from sea to shining sea. What an adventure that was, what an experience over the road trucking is.

Anyway, this book is about the 1990s, and all my experiences therein. I'm only writing this book because everyone I know tells me, if you write a biography about your life, you can only write one book. They say that no one has ever written (two) books about themselves. So, just as I have been doing my entire life, I'm proving them all to be wrong and I will probably write a third one someday. Please enjoy.

(Back!) Again

In 1991, I was 23 years old and working at a Buick dealership in Oklahoma City. I had been working at this dealership for about a year and a half. I was in college and trying to get my associate degree in science and auto mechanics, and I was a full-time student at Oklahoma City Community College. I had previously taken two years of auto mechanics in high school at the Vo-Tech. I was now trying to get certified as an ASE auto mechanic, with an associate degree (in science), to back it up. I went to school each day until three o'clock, then I went to work at the Buick dealership until seven or eight o'clock each evening. I also worked all day on Saturday at the dealership. So, I was a full-time student and I got about 30 hours each week at the dealership.

The plan was to get through the two-year program at college and get my degree. While working just enough at the dealer to pay the bills at my little one-room apartment and pay my tuition at school. This plan had been working out great for about a year and a half, I was only about six months away from graduating and getting my degree.

I liked working at the dealership, I learned a lot about cars from all the other mechanics who worked there. The first year that I worked at the Buick dealership, all I did was run the lube rack. This meant I just changed the oil and did an occasional transmission service. I also got to do a few coolant flushes and tire rotate and balances when the other guys were too busy. But most of the time during that first year, I just changed the oil in people's cars.

The last six months I worked there, they had moved me over to the (front end and brake) man. They brought in a trainer from a local school and spent a whole Saturday teaching me how to run the front-end alignment machine. It was an old (Bear) front end alignment machine that was built back in the '70s. It wasn't electronic, like modern front end alignment machines. It worked by using mirrors and leveling bubbles, I found it simple to operate. I loved the work and really enjoyed doing front end and brake work.

As you know with your own car. front end alignment and brakes are very, very important for your car to operate properly and safely. I worked the front-end alignment machine and fixed people's brakes for about six months. What a job, I loved it, and it paid about twice as much as I had been making running the lube rack and changing the oil. I was doing great and saving money for the future. I only had about six months to go to finish college and get my degree. If you read my other book, you already know that I had gotten a girl pregnant in high school and was already divorced and paying child support on my daughter Melissa by this time.

One dreadful Saturday morning everything changed. I was working in the shop, just like I had for the past year and a half on Saturdays, and on Saturdays, I was the only one in the shop all the other mechanics were off on Saturday, they only worked on weekdays. The owner of the dealership (Pete) had been arguing

15

for weeks with the oldest, and most tenured mechanic we had in our shop (Paul).

Paul was about 60 years old and had been working at the dealership ever since it opened, over 20 years ago. He was probably the best mechanic in our shop. All of us other mechanics, if we were stumped, or just couldn't figure out what was wrong with a car. We could always go to Paul and find the answer, or at least get some very good advice. You know the guy, the smartest person in the shop, which is usually the oldest guy in the shop, well, that was Paul at our shop. He was very wise and had seen it all in his 20 plus years at the Buick dealership. The problem was Paul didn't have any book smarts; he didn't even have a high school diploma. Even though he was the smartest mechanic in our shop, he couldn't pass a written test if his life depended on it.

In the '90s most shops started phasing out all the old shade tree types of mechanics, and only hiring ASE certified mechanics. Paul told me he had taken the written test over 15 times in the past four or five years, and he just couldn't pass it and get his certification. No matter how hard he studied, and no matter how much he knew about working on cars. When you put it down on paper, he just didn't get it, and he would fail the written exam time and time again.

Every time Paul failed the test he would get into another huge argument with Pete, the owner of the shop. I believe Pete really liked Paul and wanted him to get certified and continue working there, after all, Paul was his oldest employee. The problem was Pete could no longer have uncertified mechanics working in his shop. I believe this new protocol of not having non-certified mechanics in your shop, was put in place by the auto manufacturers themselves, and the insurance companies.

I still to this day don't think it was fair to the old school guys who lost their jobs in those years just because they didn't have the book smarts to pass the written test and get certified, some of those guys were the best mechanics around at that time.

So anyway, after another failed written test, and another huge fight with Pete, on Friday,

Paul was fired from the Buick dealership, where I worked. Paul came to the shop early that Saturday morning to pick up his toolbox, and all his tools. He had one of those giants (Snap-On), upright, rollaway toolboxes, and you can only imagine the number of tools he had acquired after being on the job for over 20 years. He owned every tool they had ever made, and this thing was humongous and very, very heavy, I bet it weighed over 500 pounds.

  Paul drove a little, single cab S-10 pickup. When he showed up that Saturday morning to get his toolbox, I was the only person working in the shop. It didn't really matter, even if the shop had been full of guys, I would have been the first person to offer to help him because Paul was probably my favorite person working in that shop. He had shown me and taught me so much about working on cars in the past year and a half, that I could never do enough to repay him.

  Anyway, as I said, I was the only one in the shop that dreadful Saturday morning. So as soon as I saw him pull his pickup inside, I went over and started helping him load his tools into the back of it. We got all the small stuff loaded up and quickly realized we needed help loading that giant roll away toolbox.

I considered myself to be a big strong guy. I was always working out. Paul, on the other hand, was like 60 years old and pretty skinny looking. There was no way he could pick up one side of that giant toolbox and load it into his pickup. So, I ran up to the body shop, which was just up the hill behind our shop. I got some kid from the body shop to come down and help us load the toolbox.

Paul and the kid from the body shop got on one side, and I got on the other side. About halfway up into the back of Paul's pick up we all heard a loud POP! noise, come from my back. It was a very loud (POP), kind of like when you pop your knuckles, but much, much louder. I wasn't about to drop that giant toolbox on those guys, so, I just gritted my teeth and went on up into the back of the truck with severe pain.

As soon as I let go of the toolbox, I screamed in pain! I didn't know it yet, but I had broken my back in three places and pinched a nerve going to my left leg. I crushed two disks in my back and ruptured a third disk. I pinched the sciatic nerve going to my left leg. I was in immediate pain! I couldn't walk or bend my back. If I did, I could feel the pieces of the broken disk, rubbing together and pinching that nerve.

This was the most pain I had ever felt, even after my kidney stones and my motorcycle wreck and getting thrown out of the back of a pickup on a paved highway at 65 miles an hour and getting hit in the head with an axe. (Read the first book). This was still the most painful thing I had ever felt.

I went inside and told the supervisor, I hurt my back loading Paul's toolbox, and I needed to go home for the day. I thought I had just pulled a muscle or something. I thought I could just go home and rest and then go to school and work on Monday, Man was I wrong. Every day it just got worse and worse; I couldn't even walk by Monday. The pinched nerve pain was so bad I could not stand it. Plus, I could feel those pieces of disk scraping together every time I tried to take a step; the pain was excruciating!

I'm telling you guys, pinched nerve pain is way, way worse than kidney stone pain and the funny part is, the doctor told me that kidney stone pain is the closest a man can ever come to actual labor pain. Which is supposed to be the worst kind of pain there is, but a pinched nerve in your back is much worse, trust me.

If you knew me at all, you would know that I hate to go to the doctor. I will only go if I can't breathe or can't walk or can't get out of bed. So, I didn't go to the doctor for almost two weeks. I was hoping my back would get to feeling better and I could get back to school and work, however, it did not, it just continued to get worse and worse. After two weeks I could no longer stand the pain and I had no choice but to go to the doctor. The strongest pain pills I could find weren't doing anything for the pain.

I had been checking in with my supervisor every couple of days, he had been telling me to wait a few more days, if I could, and see if it got any better. Looking back now, I think he was just worried about a lawsuit. He was just looking out for the company, and not really looking out for my wellbeing. I probably should have gone to the emergency room that very first day, hindsight though, right?

When I did finally go to the doctor, they did an MRI and a Myelogram. They said I had two crushed disks, another ruptured disk, and a pinched nerve going to my left leg. They said I needed to have immediate, major back surgery.

I went home to think before deciding to let them cut into my back. All I knew was that I couldn't walk, and I couldn't stand the horrible pain, I went home and called my supervisor again. He said, "Go get a second opinion, maybe you don't really need back surgery". I was young and naïve, but I realized right then that he wasn't on my side at all, and I decided to call a lawyer.

I was worried because I didn't have any health insurance. I was a part-time employee and didn't get any benefits. The lawyer said to go ahead and schedule the surgery and not to worry about the hospital bills or anything else. He said the dealership was responsible for my hospital bills and my time off work. So, I scheduled the surgery, but I wasn't sure I could go through with it. I had never had actual surgery before or been under the knife, so to speak. To say the least, I was absolutely scared to death.

I went to the hospital the day the surgery was scheduled. I limped in and sat down in the waiting room and spent about 20 minutes filling out paperwork. I was so nervous that I did not want to be there at all. Finally, they took my paperwork, and a nurse came and got me and took me into a changing room. She gave me a funny looking gown thing and told me to strip down and put it on. The whole time I was thinking I don't want to be here, and I don't want to do this. I was praying for God to heal my back so I wouldn't have to go through with this surgery. Please, please God anything so I won't have to let these people cut into my back.

When she left the room, I threw the gown thing on a chair and limped back to my truck and took off. By the time I got home the doctor had already called and left three messages on my machine. "Where did you go, what happened", he asked?... I waited until the next day to return his call, so I could think about it, I told him I chickened out and went home. He said, "You need to have this surgery, it's an emergency!" I said, "Okay, let's reschedule it and I will come back".

Three or four days later, I went back for my second scheduled back surgery appointment. This time after the waiting room, they got me into a gown and upstairs into a room. I was laying in the bed and had an I.V. in my arm, so they could give me medication. I was so nervous, again I didn't want to be there, I didn't want them cutting into me. The nurse came in and asked me if I was comfortable. I said, "HELL NO! I hate this place". I said, "I can't even stand the smell of this place".

She said, "I'll be back in a few minutes with the doctor. Then we can go over the procedure we will be performing on you today". As soon as she left the room, I jumped up and yanked the I.V. out of my arm and got dressed. I again limped back to my truck and drove home.

Again, they called and called, until three days later when I finally answered the phone. The doctor said, "Listen, this is very important. If you don't have this surgery and fix your back, you may never be able to walk right again". He said, "You must come back and have this surgery". I said, "Okay doc, here's what we got to do". I said, "As soon as I come inside the door to the hospital, I want you to set me down in a wheelchair and knock me out. When I wake up, I want the surgery to be all over with". He said, "Okay, let's make you another appointment".

So, a couple of days later I went to the hospital for my third back surgery appointment. As soon as I entered the front door, they put me into a wheelchair and gave me something to knock me out. When I woke up the surgery was all over with.

They took the two crushed disks completely out of my back, making me almost an inch shorter than I used to be. The doctor said since I was so young, the muscles would grow around the missing disk, and I would be fine. He repaired the ruptured disk and said the pinched nerve should heal up on its own, now that he had removed the broken pieces that were pinching against it.

I was in the hospital for almost a week, I could just barely stand up or even walk one step at all in the first days after the surgery. I couldn't put any weight on my left leg for a long time. I went to physical therapy for a year and a half, learning how to walk again. For a long time, my left leg wouldn't work right because of the damage to the nerve. It took months and months of stretching and doing exercises to get my leg to work right again.

I don't know if you guys have ever had to learn how to walk again, or not. But I'm here to tell y'all, it is much harder to learn the second time around. The first time I learned to walk, I just pulled my 22-pound body up on the side of the sofa and took a few steps as I waddled along the side of the couch. Probably giggling and cooing and having a good old time. However, the second time I learned how to walk was a different story altogether.

First, I weighed closer to 175 and had to pull myself out of a wheelchair, not just up along the side of the sofa. If I had my druthers, I would prefer to use the 22-pound version of myself and pull it up alongside the sofa for a few steps. Trust me when I tell you, that you would probably feel the same way. Because the second time I learned how to walk there was a God-awful amount of (PAIN!) involved with every step, and I can assure you there was (NO!) giggling or cooing involved.

After a year and a half of physical therapy and rehab, I was ready to return to work. The problem was, during the year and a half I was learning to walk again. Pete, the guy who owned the Buick dealership where I had worked (retired). Pete's son took over the business during my time off. I was told later that Pete's son only ran the business for about six months before they ran out of money and closed the doors.

During my year and a half off work I had used all my workman's comp benefits, which lasted only six months. I then used all my unemployment benefits, that also lasted another six months. Then I had been living off my savings for the final six months, and my savings were also all gone now. I didn't know what to do, I was broke, and now I didn't even have a job to go back to. So, I asked the lawyer, "What do I do now?"

He said now that I had finally been released by the doctor the dealership's insurance would pay all my medical bills and we could sue them for my time off work. I said, "Great! Let's go to court, I'm broke, " He said, "Okay". So, a few weeks later we went to court, I was scared to death. The judge put me on the stand to talk about the whole traumatic experience of breaking my back and spending a year and a half learning how to walk again.

I was very nervous and shaking as I did my best to describe the whole experience. I told the judge how I had broken my back lifting a very large toolbox. I told him I heard it (pop) and should have dropped the toolbox immediately, but I couldn't drop it on Paul and that kid. So, I gritted my teeth and completed the job. Most of the damage to the nerve was probably done after I gritted my teeth and went on up into the truck.

Then I described the three trips to the hospital and the back surgery that followed. Then I spent 20 minutes describing what it took to teach my left leg how to walk again, and all the months I had spent in physical therapy.

This was just a hearing though. After I finished, I went and sat down by my lawyer. The company's lawyer then got up and started talking to the judge. He said the insurance company wanted to settle out of court, or without going to trial. He said they would pay all my medical bills and give me $15,000 for my time off work. My lawyer asked me if I wanted to just take the $15k and be done with it or stay the course and fight them. I said, "I'm completely broke, I don't have a job or any money to pay my rent". I said, "I'll take the $15k, write me a check". After paying court costs and attorney fees, I got just over $11,000.

I was off work for a year and a half, I had to learn how to walk again. That was the end of my mechanic career, and I never went back to college or got my degree, I settled out of court for $11k. If this incident would have never happened, I would have easily made four or five times that amount if I had just kept on working for that year and a half, you talk about a life-altering event.

I never worked as an automotive mechanic again, and I never went back and finished college. The doctor later told me I was 55% disabled in my back and I needed to go back to school and get a desk job. He told me I would never be able to lift over 15 pounds for the rest of my life. He said I would never be able to do manual labor or spend all day bent over the hood of a car, so my mechanic career was over before it started.

A few years after that, I (*actually*) set records in the weight room I used to work out in. I have bench pressed 400 pounds and squatted close to 600 pounds after I broke my back. There is still a plaque on the wall with my name on it where I used to workout. Not bad for a guy who's 5 foot 4 inches and weighs 175 pounds, with a bad back.

It is all in your mind, you can do anything you set your mind to. If you are willing to put in the work and never give up on your dreams. The human body is a magnificent machine. You just need to get off the couch and be willing to push it to the limit. You just must keep pushing forward and never give up.

Now that I am 50 years old, my back bothers me a lot. I have a lot of arthritis and the sciatic nerve in my left leg still bothers me a lot, but I tell my kids all the time, you can do anything you set your mind to, just never give up. I recently re-roofed and repainted our entire house all by myself. Just keep moving forward, and never say never.......T.J.

Chapter 2
Not an Auto Mechanic!

What if you had spent your whole life wanting to be an auto mechanic? What if you had been working on cars ever since you were 12 or 13 years old? What if you had taken two years of auto mechanics in high school and another year and a half in college? What if you had worked at two dealerships and all your dreams and thoughts were, that you would spend your life as an automotive mechanic? What if all your friends were auto mechanics? What if you had spent your life collecting an almost unimaginable wealth of hand tools? (That you no longer needed). What if all your dreams, goals, and desires, for the past 10 years, had been aimed at the automotive technician industry? Then. What if you woke up one morning and realized, you would never make a living as an auto mechanic again? Now, what do you do, where do you turn, who do you call? Where do you even begin?

I was thinking, what's next? My whole life I have been thinking, "what's next!" Every time in my life when I was down and out and not sure where to turn. I always look on the bright side and think, okay "What's Next"? A new adventure. A new path to follow, maybe a new job, a new career, a new way of thinking.

I just start aiming my mind at, what's next? This keeps me from getting depressed or down and out and never getting off the couch. Imagine if we never got off the couch and searched for (What's next?). We would never find it and our life would be empty. So, I motivated myself and went in search of what's next. I just started going around town filling out applications, looking for a new job.

I could have felt sorry for myself and stayed on the couch for another year, but I didn't. I self-motivated and went in search of a new adventure. I filled out tons of applications and searched every day through the want ads in the newspaper. What's next, what's next? The doctor had told me I could not lift over 15 pounds, and I still only had about 75% use of my left leg and bad back, I wasn't sure what I could even do. I had never worked in fast food or worked a cash register before. All my jobs had been manual labor type jobs that involved a lot of bending and lifting. Now I needed something where you just sit there or stand there and run a machine or something. I wasn't exactly sure what that was going to be. Maybe something on an assemble line or in a machine shop.

It took several weeks of driving around filling out applications, doing interviews and talking to people. Then one day I had a brilliant idea. What if I could drive a delivery truck that didn't involve heavy lifting? Then I figured it out, (a bus), go drive a bus. I went to the nearest school and sure enough, they were begging for school bus drivers. They needed drivers so bad, that they were willing to train you and help you get your CDL license, it was perfect, I could just sit in the seat and drive. How easy is that? After three weeks of training, I received my class (B)

CDL. A Commercial Driver's License with a passenger endorsement, I was now a bus driver.

I soon had two jobs, I drove a school bus and I drove an elderly bus for the community center. School bus drivers go to work every morning between 6 and 8 am. Then they go back and run the evening route between 3 and 5 pm. The elderly bus ran from 9 to 2 every day, it was perfect. I had two jobs and made a pretty good living. The kids were pretty good most of the time, and the elderly people just loved me. It was a great adventure for me. I think everyone should have to drive a school bus for a while, it puts everything in perspective.

After about a year though, I was bored and looking for a new adventure in my life. I later drove a trolley and a city transit bus for a while. Just trying to figure out what I wanted to do with my life, and always looking for "What's Next".

I spent about four months driving a trolley. During those four months, one evening I took a trolley load of women to a bachelorette

36

party. I went to the bus barn to pick up my trolley, then as always, I completed my pre-trip inspection. I checked the tires and all the lights. Then I checked all the fluid levels and fired the trolley up. Then I made sure the CB radio and air conditioning were working properly. You always check your radio before you leave the shop just in case you need to radio for help. Then I drove to the pickup address and picked up the 14 women.

You talk about a rowdy bunch, these women were already drinking, and ready to party. I was thinking, these 14 women can make more noise than 50 or 60 regular passengers. They were all singing and dancing on the trolley. They didn't set down for one minute on the entire trip. I took them to a strip club in Oklahoma City that usually had women dancers. But tonight, they were having an all-male review, with only male strippers. They asked me if I would like to go inside with them, I said, "I don't think so. I will just wait outside. " I asked them how long they would be inside, they said, at least two or three hours.

So, I said I might go get something to eat while I was waiting, but I would be back before they were finished. I told them to have fun, and as soon as they were out of the trolley, I drove off. I wasn't sure what I could do to kill two or three hours, but I wasn't interested in staying at this place. So, I drove over to a little restaurant where I had eaten before, I went inside and had a nice dinner. I still had another two hours before I had to be back at the strip club. So, I decided to take the long way back and drive around the city for a while.

    I got onto the highway and had only gone a few miles when I passed a guy who was walking down the right-hand side of the highway. There was a get-on ramp just right beside the guy walking, where cars were coming up onto the highway. It was just getting dark, and it was hard to see the guy walking down the shoulder of the road.

    Just as I drove past the man walking one of the cars coming up the get-on ramp, (Hit!) the man that was walking. I saw the guy go flying into the air and go tumbling completely over the top of the car. The guy landed on the pavement, on the shoulder of the highway. I couldn't believe my eyes; I couldn't believe what I just saw. It looked like something you would only see in a cartoon, or on a stunt show. I hesitated for a minute because it just didn't seem real. The car that hit the guy who was walking, was now speeding away and in the process of passing my trolley.

I could see in my rearview mirror that several cars had already stopped to try and help the man who had been run over. I made a split-second decision to chase after the car, instead of pulling over to try and help. The only problem was that I was driving a slow-moving trolley and the car was disappearing in front of me. I hit the gas pedal and went as fast as the trolley would go.

Finally, after what seemed like an eternity, I caught up with the car. The driver of the car quickly realized he was being followed and started darting in and out of traffic, I followed him as best as I could. The car was driving ninety miles an hour and weaving in and out of traffic. The car then took an exit and went downtown. I followed him, not sure what I was going to do if the guy stopped.

At a stoplight, I pulled up beside the car and yelled to the guy to pull over, but the guy just ignored me and kept on going. At the next light, again I pulled up beside him and yelled "Pull Over! Pull Over!" I was thinking maybe I could make a citizen's arrest or something. Just then, the guy made a quick U-turn and got back up onto the highway. I couldn't turn the trolley on a dime as the car did. I had to pull into a parking lot and turn around. By the time I got back up onto the highway, the car was nowhere in sight.

I drove as fast as that trolley would go for almost five miles. Then I spotted the little red car just a few cars ahead of me. I tried to creep up behind the guy, to hopefully not be noticed. I was thinking this time if I could get close enough, I would just get the guy's tag number and call the police, but just as I was closing in on the guy, he noticed me in his rearview mirror and took off again. I chased him for another 15 minutes, weaving in and out of traffic. Then the guy took another exit. I was thinking, 'I got you now', because you will have to stop at a red light, and I can get your tag number this time. I dialed 911 and was explaining the situation to the operator.

When just then the guy had to stop at a red light, I read his tag number to the operator and gave them our location. Within about three minutes there was a cop car right behind me, with all its lights and sirens blasting. After a few more minutes three or four police cars were chasing behind me.

Then I finally decided to pull over and give up the pursuit. I had been following the car for almost an hour. Three of the police cars continued the pursuit of the car, and the other one pulled over with me. I told the entire story to the officer, who confirmed it with his dispatcher. Then the police officer had me fill out and sign a report. At that point, I was free to go.

I drove back to the club, where I had dropped the busload of women a few hours earlier, I waited outside until they came out. I was too embarrassed to go inside the club. After collecting the women from the club, I took them to a restaurant for dinner. You talk about a noisy bunch of girls. They sang and danced again, all the way to the restaurant. Most of them had been drinking at the club and I got a good laugh out of watching them act like fools. Again, I just waited outside while the women had dinner.

    During this time, I called the police station and asked if the guy who was run over had survived his injuries, and if the driver of the little red car had been caught. The police dispatcher told me that the guy who was run over was transported to the hospital by a concerned citizen, and he had two broken legs and some other small wounds, but he was expected to recover. Also, the dispatcher said, that thanks to all my efforts, the driver of the red car had been arrested and taken to jail. They said I might be called in later to testify if there was a hearing on all of this. The dispatcher thanked me for all my help. Then I asked for the guy's name who had been run over. I thought maybe I would try and go visit him in the hospital.

A few days later I went and visited the guy in the hospital. He was very thankful for everything he had heard that I had done to help catch the guy who hit him. I told him the entire story of how I chased the guy down with a 26-passenger trolley. I said, "Thank God I didn't have any passengers at the time". We got a good laugh out of it. He said he was going to have to have surgery on one of his legs, but the doctor said it should be fine. It looked to me like he would be okay after a few months of recovery.

Finally, after what seemed like forever. The women came out of the restaurant, and I drove them back to the house where I had picked them up from earlier that evening. As they were getting off the trolley one of them said, "Man, you sure got a boring job". Little did she know? Right? The last lady off my trolley was the main lady who had set up this whole trip. As she staggered out the door, she handed me a (tip). I said, "Thank you very much, ma'am, goodnight". Then after she was out the door, I counted the wad of money she had just handed me. It was $32, all in one-dollar bills. I laughed out loud as I thought it must have been leftover ones, they were stuffing down some guy's shorts at that club. How funny right? Then I returned the trolley to the bus barn. When I got home, I was totally exhausted. I thought, what a day! What a day…

In 1994 I found myself in between jobs again. I had decided to try some local delivery truck type of work and had been filling out applications for about a week at different delivery truck type places. I had a class (B) CDL license with a passenger endorsement. So, I could legally drive anything under 26,000 pounds, or anything with passengers. I was thinking maybe a local delivery truck, or dump truck or something.

One day I stopped at this welding shop, pipe yard, looking place. I went in and asked for the manager. I asked him if he needed any kind of delivery driver. He said, "No, but we do need a guy to move the pipe around in the yard". I said "I'm sorry, I would love to, but I have a bad back. For the past couple of years, I have been driving for a living." I told him I had a class (B) CDL driver's license. Then I said, "Thank you anyway", and I turned around and started walking away. He said, "Hang on a minute, have you ever thought of going to truck driving school and getting a class (A) CDL license?" He said, "I know a guy who recently went and he's now doing great (over the road trucking). He makes a lot of money and gets to travel around and see the whole countryside".

My problem was, we were in Oklahoma City at the time, and the nearest truck driving school was in St. Louis Missouri. (It's crazy, because nowadays there is a truck driving school right here in Oklahoma City). Plus, I was pretty much broke and couldn't figure out how to get myself to St. Louis, much less come up with the $2500 for the three-week truck driver training school.

So, I took a job driving a local concrete delivery truck (mixer), I didn't really like this job though. The company I worked for had the oldest, ugliest trucks you ever saw. The truck I drove was so old and broken that nothing on it ever seemed to work right. It was an absolute fight every day to try and get the job done with that old broken-down equipment that should have been in the scrap metal pile years ago.

I only drove the concrete mixer for three months. I was trying to save up some money to get myself to St. Louis and go to truck driver training school. During these three months, I was homeless. My lease had run out in the little apartment I was renting. I didn't want to renew the lease because I knew I was going to St. Louis as soon as possible. So, I just lived in an old 1978 Chevy Blazer that I was driving at the time.

I took the back seat out and welded two six-foot-long pieces of angle iron across the Blazer where the seat used to be. I put plywood down and made a foam mattress there. I slept in the Blazer every night during these three months and saved my money. I had a membership at a local gym where I would go and work out every day after working at the concrete company. After my workout, I would shower there at the gym.

Then I would drive out to the city lake and park and get some sleep in that old Blazer.

When I quit the concrete company and headed for St. Louis, I had a little over $600 to my name. You talk about (What's Next), and a new adventure. I had never been to St. Louis before, but I was glad to be finished driving that old worn-out concrete mixer for minimum wage, and I was ready for a new adventure.

I called and enrolled myself in the truck driving school and had three days to get there before the class I was in started. I was driving that old 1978 Chevy blazer that was on its last leg. I wasn't sure if it would even make the 500-mile trip from Oklahoma City to St. Louis Missouri, but I filled up the tank and took off up the highway. All my tires were bald, and I blew out two tires on the trip. Somehow, by the grace of God, I made it to St. Louis on time.

I only had enough money for gas and food for the three weeks I was at the school. So, I slept in that old Chevy Blazer in their parking lot for three weeks because I didn't have any money to get a room. I went to the classroom every day for 8 hours. Then I would go out to my Blazer and spend the evenings studying the textbooks, before falling asleep.

I had to go down the road to eat every day. I only ate once a day, at an all you can eat buffet place. I guarantee you I got my $8 worth at that buffet once a day. Then I would drive back to the school parking lot and get some sleep. It was in October, and I can tell you guys that St. Louis is very cold in October. I just about froze to death sleeping in that parking lot for three or four weeks in that old Blazer. I had a small TV in the back of that Blazer, and back then you could still use (rabbit ears) to pick up the local news stations. So, I could watch the news in the evenings.

I practiced and practiced and practiced, I would stay up half the night studying. At the end of the class, I got a 98 on the written exam and a 95 on the driving exam. The instructor called me into his office and gave me a special achievement award for having the top grade in the class.

I didn't know it, but no one can ever fail at a truck driver training school. There were several students in my class that had been there for months and months. If you don't pass the written or driving test, you can just stay there as long as it takes and keep on retaking the test until you pass and get your license. No wonder there are so many drivers on the road that don't know how to drive, right? Some of those students took several months to take a three-week class :)

I however, got mine on the first try. I stayed for another week, while I was waiting for a trucking company to put me to work. Once you got your license, the driving school would help you find a driving job. So, I stayed at the school an extra week while they helped me find a driving job. I didn't have anywhere else to go anyway.

During that week I helped some of the other students learning how to back, park, and drive, the 75-foot-long truck. It was easy to drive for me because I had already driven buses and concrete trucks and all kinds of other trucks before. Most of those students had never driven anything bigger than a Volkswagen before, and there was a huge learning curve.

Anyway, I got my first trucking job from an outfit in Arkansas (PAM trucking). I left the school in St. Louis and drove straight to the (PAM yard) in Arkansas, in that old Chevy Blazer. When I got to PAM, I had three days of orientation. Then they would put all new drivers into a truck with a so-called (trainer). You would drive around with a trainer for two or three weeks before getting your own truck.

The guy they stuck me with was a chain-smoking, coffee guzzling, swearing, cussing, insomniac. I was a good driver, and I knew it. I could have easily just gotten into a truck without a trainer and been just fine. I had been driving trucks for a living for several years already, just in smaller trucks. I did not need to be trained, certainly not by this guy.

I just needed to learn how to fill out the logbook and do the other paperwork. I didn't need any help with driving or handling the truck.

The problem was, all this guy did was yell at me, constantly, he never slept and drank coffee by the gallon. He chain-smoked all day and all night; he constantly had a lit cigarette in his hand. I don't smoke and I hated it. He would get on a caffeine high and be bouncing off the walls of the truck, he would scream and cuss me daily. It's funny because today I don't even remember that guy's name.

    His main problem was, I hated to double clutch, I only used the clutch to stop and start. When I'm driving, I don't use the clutch to shift gears. He liked to double-clutch and wanted me to. He would scream and cuss me every day for not using the clutch. He would get mad and start throwing things around in the truck. One time he *(actually)* threw the map at me while I was driving, the big heavy Rand McNally Truckers Road map.

    It was a full-size sleeper truck, with a full-size bed on the bottom and a twin size fold up bed on the top. However, there's still not a lot of room in there for two people to live together. He would get to bouncing off the walls and throwing a fit and drive me nuts. He was the worst so-called (trainer), I ever heard of. One time he had been screaming at me all day and I wanted to just quit and go home. I decided to just get in my bunk and let him drive all day while I slept. I was hoping he would cool down and chill out, but he did not. I believe it was about midnight when he started yelling for me to get my lazy (blank), out of bed.

I had been sleeping for six or seven hours and just let him drive. I got up and came up front and sat down in the passenger seat. He was cussing and screaming at me while I put my boots on. It was dark outside, and we were just pulling into a giant warehouse place where we were supposed to deliver our trailer.

I had no idea where we were because I had been asleep for so long. All I knew was we were in Indiana when I stopped driving. So, I thought we were somewhere in Ohio now. It was dark and we were in an industrial area on the outskirts of a big city, you could see the city lights off in the distance. I didn't know it yet but the city off in the distance was Columbus Ohio.

We pulled into the warehouse parking lot. The crazy, (trainer) guy went inside to turn in our paperwork and ask where they wanted the trailer parked. As soon as he got out of the truck, I grabbed the Qualcomm and typed out a message to our dispatcher. Qualcomm is a satellite driven device truckers use to keep in contact with their dispatcher through. I typed this message.

"To whom it may concern. I can't take this crazy trainer guy cussing and screaming at me anymore. If I stay in this truck one more day, I will end up killing him, T.J." ... I then pushed SEND.

Then I grabbed my overnight bag and jumped out of the truck. I started walking towards those city lights. I had no idea where I was at, or where I was going. I just knew, if I stayed in that truck any longer, I was going to end up hurting that old crazy guy. I had been in his truck for about a week, and I'd had all I could take, of his screaming and throwing things at me. So, I started walking towards those city lights. It looked like two or three miles away in the dark but ended up being more like six or eight miles to the city. It took me nearly two hours to walk to the nearest store that I could find open.

I walked into the parking lot where there was a guy pumping gas into his car. I said, "Hey man, where are we?" He looked at me really funny, as if I had just fallen off of a UFO or something, and said, "What do you mean?" Again, I said, "Where are we? What is the name of this town?" He said, "Columbus, why?" I said, "Columbus Ohio?" He said, "Hell yeah, what other Columbus would it be?" I said, "Thank you", and turned and started walking away.

Then I suddenly turned back and said, "Hey, which way is south?" Again, he looked at me as if I were totally insane and said, "What do you mean"? I said, "Which way is south, man?" He pointed to his left and I started walking. That guy must have thought I just fell off another planet or something, he gave me the funniest look I've ever seen on another human being. I guess when I just walked up in the dark, in the middle of the night it must have looked crazy to him. (I still laugh every time I think about it).

I asked him which way south was because if I was going to walk back to Oklahoma City, I didn't want to start off walking the wrong direction. I did not want to find out the next morning that I had been walking north and was practically in Canada. Without the sun, I had no idea which way was what.

I ended up walking around Columbus for a couple of hours asking people where the bus station was at. I got to the bus station just before daylight. I had a little less than $200 in my pocket. Thank God the ticket to Oklahoma City was like $150 bucks. However, I had to wait for like 6 hours to catch the next bus going that way.

Then I had to change buses three times along the way. It took two days to get to Oklahoma City on the bus. I changed buses in Indianapolis, with a two-hour layover. Then I had to go to Chicago, which was totally out of the way and change buses again with another layover. Then I went to St. Louis where I had a four-hour layover before going on to Oklahoma City.

I spent those four hours walking around downtown St. Louis. I went over and saw the river and riverboats, then I went and checked out the Arch. I went up to the top and the view was pretty cool. It was, all in all, boring though. It's supposed to be the gateway to the west, but when I walked under it, I didn't feel any different. All my life people made it sound like a Disney ride or something, but it seemed kind of ho-hum to me, it is huge though.

I had just been to St. Louis two weeks earlier. When I spent a month at the truck driver training school, but I never had time to see St. Louis because I was always busy at the driving school. So, it was kind of nice to spend those four hours in downtown St. Louis.

When I got home my dispatcher had already been calling my friends and family trying to get ahold of me. I called PAM and told them what had happened. I told them that the trainer guy was crazy, and I couldn't work with him any longer. I said if I had stayed in his truck any longer, I would have ended up hurting him. I told them how he cussed me and threw things in the truck; I said the guy was dangerous.

Three days later they sent another trainer guy to pick me up on his way through Oklahoma City, and they reimbursed me for my bus ticket and apologized for the crazy guy. The new trainer (Dave) was awesome, he didn't smoke, or cuss and we got along great.

I only drove with Dave for 4 or 5 days. We left Oklahoma City, went to Laredo Texas, and picked up a load and took it to the PAM yard in Arkansas. Dave let me drive every inch of the way. He told me I was the best student driver he had ever had. and he said he could tell I had driven trucks before. He said some people double-clutch when they shift, and some don't.

He said it works either way, just whatever you prefer and you're more comfortable with. I drove the entire trip, backing and parking and driving the truck. When we got to the PAM yard in Arkansas, Dave went inside and told dispatch to give me my *(own)* truck. He said I was one of the best student drivers they had ever had. He said I could handle the truck as well as he could, and he had been on the job for eight years.

Thanks, Dave for being one of the good guys! Before Dave left the yard, he took me out and showed me how to put snow chains on the truck. I remember two pieces of advice Dave gave me. He said, never get in a big hurry and drive faster than the conditions allow, and never, never, go to sleep in the driver's seat of your truck!

He said he knew a guy who died one time, just sitting in the driver's seat in a rest area, (parked). He said the guy was sitting in the driver's seat with his parking brake set and he went to sleep. He was parked right behind another truck in a rest area. He must have woken up at some point in the night and had a heart attack when he saw he was only a few inches from the truck in front of him. He gripped the steering wheel and slammed on the brakes with all his might. He must have thought he was still out on the road driving and had fallen asleep at the wheel. Dave said when they found the guy they had to (pry) his hands off the steering wheel. So, Dave said never, never, sleep in the driver's seat. Period!

The next morning PAM trucking gave me my very own truck to drive. It was a brand-new Freightliner rig, with all the bells and whistles. It was brand new; no one had ever driven it before. It had less than 20 miles on the odometer. It was a full-size sleeper, with a full-size bed on the bottom and a twin size fold away sleeper on the top. It had a small television and even a small microwave oven.

You could stand up and walk around in this truck, it was magnificent, and I thought it was beautiful. It had a 10-speed transmission with a splitter for high and low. It had a beautiful caterpillar diesel engine with two 60-gallon fuel tanks. I could drive over 1000 miles without stopping for fuel, this truck was awesome. I now had a new job that I loved, and a new house to live in, all in one. You talk about a new adventure! I was riding high. Woo-Hoo, here we go!

Before they turned me loose with their brand-new truck, I had to drive it 5 miles with a supervisor in the truck. He ran me through an obstacle course there in the yard. He made me stop, back, dock, and parallel park it. Then he took me out on the road for a 5-mile drive. Piece of cake, I loved that brand new truck, it was the coolest thing I had ever driven. When we got back to the yard, he said 'Thank you and be careful out there'... and down the road, I went. To a wonderful new adventure with the whole world in front of my windshield.

Chapter 3
On The Road Again

My first load was a trailer full of diapers, for Walmart. The trailer was sitting in our yard in Arkansas, needed to be delivered to Philadelphia, Pennsylvania. I guess they must use a lot of diapers in Philadelphia. The good thing about hauling diapers is they don't weigh anything. You can stuff that 53-foot trailer completely full of diapers and it feels like you are dragging an empty trailer. Very easy work for the driver and the truck. However, I had never been to Philadelphia before. This was going to be a new experience for sure.

During the two years I worked for PAM, 90% of my loads were either for Walmart or General Motors. The whole two years I was on 'General Freight'. This means I didn't have a dedicated run from one place to another. Every time I got a new load, I was going to a new place I had never been before. It was like Christmas time, opening a new present. I would open the Qualcomm and say, "Okay, where are we going today?" A lot of guys prefer to be on a dedicated run, so they know exactly where they are going every day, but I loved being on general freight and getting to go to a new town every trip. It was exciting, going to a new town every trip and getting to see places I had never seen before. What an awesome, exciting, adventure!

That very first trip, from Arkansas to Philadelphia was an exciting adventure for sure. It was in November and the snow was flying. I don't know if you guys have ever driven a 75-foot truck in the snow before, or not, but I hadn't yet, and it was about to get real.

I would find out later that even though hauling diapers is easy work, it is no good in the snow! You really want that truck as heavy as the law allows when you are driving in the snow. The truck drives and handles much better in the snow if it weighs 80,000 pounds than it does if it only weighs 50,000 pounds. I would soon find this out the hard way. The truck slips and slides and fishtails and does all kinds of weird things in the snow, when it is lightweight. So that first trip to Philadelphia was a perilous journey, to say the least.

Pennsylvania has a lot of winding, turning, and mountainous terrain, and during the '90s it seemed that every inch of it was under construction. You know those concrete barriers they use in construction zones? During the '90s we truck drivers referred to those as Pennsylvania Barricades. Even if we saw them in Texas or somewhere we called them (Pennsylvania Barricades) because they stretched across the entire state of Pennsylvania. Plus, everywhere you saw Pennsylvania Barricades the lane is only like 8 feet wide, instead of the usual 10 feet wide. This makes it very, very hard for a 75-foot truck to maneuver. Especially through those winding, turning, hilly, and mountainous, Pennsylvania roadways in the snow.

To do it safely, you must be on your toes at all times, and during the snowy months, it is ten times harder. I slipped and slid my way across Illinois, Indiana, Ohio and into

Pennsylvania, where the roads went from bad to worse. I had several near misses and saw some terrible wrecks along the way. A trip that normally took two days, ended up taking me nearly four days in the horrible, wintry conditions.

Probably the hardest part of being an over the road truck driver is the loneliness and solitude. You're in your truck 24/7 with no one to talk to. No family or friends around, and it gets lonely. You must learn to eat all your meals by yourself and *(really)* just do everything by yourself. In the mid-'90s, I didn't even carry a cell phone with me, but I'm sure truckers do nowadays.

One of the first things you learn when you become an over the road truck driver is how to talk on the CB radio. Like breaker, breaker, one nine, come on back for a radio check. The CB radio is the truck driver's most valuable tool. Next to his Rand McNally trucker's road map. You get lots of great information from the CB.

Like where the (bears) are, so you don't get a speeding ticket. Bears are cops to you guys.

Plus, lots of other good information, like where the road construction is, or where a wreck might be blocking the road before you get to it. Also, things like traffic conditions and road conditions. The CB radio is the truck driver's best friend, you can talk to other drivers about anything. You can get directions to where you're going if you are lost. Or you can just talk to someone, in the middle of the night, if you are about to fall asleep while driving, it helps you stay awake on those long road trips.

Anyway, I found on that very first trip how valuable the CB radio is to a truck driver. It told me about lots of wrecks before I got to them. It kept me abreast of the terrible road conditions that kept getting worse and worse the farther east I went. The CB even helped me find the place I was going to when I got to Philadelphia. I got lost and turned around in Philadelphia, trying to find the Walmart warehouse and deliver those diapers.

Philadelphia is humongous, and the traffic jams can be a nightmare. All the little cars zooming around everywhere and trying not to get stuck behind your 75-foot-long big truck. People will (*absolutely*) run over you trying to get out in front of you, so as not to get stuck behind a big truck, and wouldn't you know it, I passed my exit. Trying not to get ran over.

I took the next exit, which turned out to be a one-way street. I then went around the mile section three times trying to figure out how to get off that one-way street and get back to where I needed to be. I then got on my CB radio and asked for directions on how to get off this merry-go-round. Another driver told me a shortcut and an easy way to get to the Walmart warehouse. You talk about a perilous journey; man was I glad to be at Walmart finally and finished with my first load. It was an absolute miracle that I made that first delivery on time, and safely. Thank you, Jesus.

I just wanted to clarify something before I go any farther. Most of the freight I hauled during my trucking career was either for General Motors or Walmart. Now when I say, (I picked a load up at the GM plant in Texarkana Texas). I may not be talking about an actual General Motors assembly plant. I hauled windshield for General Motors that came out of Ohio, and tires for General Motors that came out of Oklahoma City, and all kinds of switches and parts that came from different (Johnson Controls) plants, scattered all across the country.

Plus. many, many other companies that make parts for General Motors. So, when I say, I picked up parts at the GM plant. It may not be an actual GM plant but just a contractor that made parts for General Motors. I could never possibly remember the names of all the companies where I picked up parts for General Motors. So, I just refer to all of them as GM plants in this book. Even though it may be a Johnson controls or a Firestone Tire or whatever.

I just don't want to get a bunch of nasty emails telling me there is (no) General Motors plant in Texarkana Texas or South Bend Indiana. I already know this, but it is much easier to just refer to them all as GM plants. Then try to name all the different sub-companies that make parts for General Motors, because trust me there are thousands....

Chapter 4
Canada 'eh?

The second load of freight I hauled for PAM trucking was for the General Motors Corporation. I went to sleep in the Walmart warehouse parking lot in Philadelphia. The next morning it was like opening Christmas presents on Christmas morning. My Qualcomm woke me up at about 6 a.m. when it beeped with a new message, and a new load to deliver. Every time I opened my Qualcomm to get a new load. I would say (out loud), "Well, where are we going today"? That was my favorite part of the job. Getting to go to a new place, I had never been before, every time I got a new load. I dropped my trailer at Walmart and picked up an empty PAM trailer.

My dispatcher had told me to (deadhead) 100 miles back west to Harrisburg Pennsylvania, for my next load. Deadheading meant you didn't have any freight and were just dragging an empty trailer, unlike (bobtailing) where do did not even have a trailer. I liked deadheading, it paid the same as hauling a load. I got paid 25 cents a mile, loaded or unloaded, but if I was just deadheading, I wasn't responsible for someone's freight and the time restraint wasn't the same. You didn't really have to hurry and get there, but the pay was the same, easy money.

    So, I got back on the interstate and headed for Harrisburg PA. In Harrisburg, I again had trouble finding the place and had to use my CB radio to get directions to the General Motors plant. When I got to the plant, I went inside to get my paperwork and find my trailer number. Again, just like opening a Christmas gift. When I got the paperwork and read that I was going to Canada to deliver car parts to another GM assembly plant, I was so excited! I had certainly never been to Canada before. What an adventure!

    Every time I got a new load and a new destination the first thing, I had to do was get out my trusty Rand McNally Truckers Road map and plan out the entire trip. I would do this each time I got a new load before I ever started rolling with it. I was so excited, man I'm going to Canada! I remember thinking maybe I will see some moose or wildlife or something. I had never seen a real moose in the wild before.

    I planned out the entire trip. As an over the road truck driver, you always try to stick to the interstates and toll roads, because you never know what kind of conditions you will run into on the smaller roads. Like a bridge, you can't cross because of weight limits, or an underpass that is too low for you to fit under. So, it's always better to just stick to interstates and toll roads.

    After you plan out your route, the second thing you must do is find the nearest truck stop and (scale-out) your load. The driver is solely responsible for the load being evenly distributed over the truck's five axles. An 18-wheeler can legally weigh up to 80,000 pounds, but you can only have 12,000 pounds on your (steering) axle. That is the front axle.

Then you should have approximately 34,000 pounds on your (drive axles), and the other 34,000 pounds on the rear trailer axles. These numbers vary based on how much weight you are hauling, but according to DOT laws, you can never have more than 12,000 pounds on your front (steering) axle. This law is in place for the safety of the trucks ability to steer properly. Plus, the front axle is the smallest axle and only has one tire on each side, unlike the rear axles that have four tires on each axle. So, for safety purposes, you have to run the truck over the scale each time you get a new load and make sure the weight is distributed properly.

In the mid-'90s, most truck stops were charging $6 to weigh your truck. Then an additional $1 for each time you want to re-weigh after you adjust your axles. I don't know what they are charging today.

There are two ways to adjust the weight distribution of your load, on an 18-wheeler. (First), the way you take the weight off the front axle is to slide the fifth wheel. The fifth wheel is a device that locks the truck and trailer together.

Most fifth wheel plates have a series of holes down the side, with a pin holding it in place. You can simply pull the pin, and with your rear trailer brakes set. You can pull the truck forward and slide the fifth wheel plate back. This will take some weight off the front axle and throw it towards the back of the truck.

(Second), Then to redistribute the weight in the trailer over the other four axles. You can slide the rear trailer axles forward or backward. The rear axles on a big truck will slide about five or six feet. This allows you to shift the weight forward or backward as needed. It works the same as sliding the fifth wheel plate. You just lock your trailer brakes and pull the pin. Then drive the truck forward or backward and reset the pin where you need it.

This procedure is fairly complicated the first few times you do it, but by your fourth or fifth load, you are an expert at it. By your tenth load, you can tell if there is too much weight on a certain axle, just by the way the truck drives and handles, but again, as the driver, you are solely responsible for making sure each load is properly distributed in weight over the truck's axles.

There are D.O.T. scales at every state line you come to. As a driver, you don't want to get a $10,000 fine because your truck weighs too much. So, you learn very early how to scale the truck out properly, and evenly.

I would leave Harrisburg and go north up through Vermont and into Canada. By the way, if you ever get a chance, Vermont is the second most beautiful state in the lower 48 states of America. In my opinion, only second to maybe the mountains around Coeur d' Alene Idaho, or maybe parts of Colorado. Only my opinion, but if you don't believe me just go to Vermont and check it out for yourself, awesome! I tell you. Anyway, I had a major surprise coming to me at the Canadian border.

By the way, I don't speak French, or Canadian, or whatever that mumbo-jumbo is they talk up there. Over on the Quebec side of Canada, they speak French Canadian. All the street signs are in French, and everyone speaks

French, at least they sure did in the '90s. They even had their own money, it's called Canadian money, and a lot of small mom and pop stores won't even take American money after you get a few miles north of the border towns.

I certainly did not have any Canadian money with me, but the money wasn't even the biggest problem. No one warned me about the rules and laws and different language or different money in Canada. PAM trucking just sent me in like it was any other load of freight, without any warnings or special instructions whatsoever.

At the border, I was (*absolutely*) violated by a couple of border guards that didn't even speak English. Or at least they never spoke English in front of me, just some crazy French-Canadian crap that I couldn't understand a single word of. When I came out of the top of Vermont and found the Canadian border. I pulled up to the border shack with no expectations of what was about to happen. It was in the middle of the night and my truck was the only vehicle in sight.

I pulled up to the guard shack and the guy said something like, "Set the brakes and get your paperwork and come inside". I'm not completely sure that's what he said. He did not speak very good English and had a very heavy French accent. I set the parking brake and went inside with my load documentation. He took my paperwork and told me to set down. He and another guy behind the counter were talking to each other in French the whole time. They took my driver's license and got on the computer, I guess to check my background or something and see if I was a wanted criminal. One guy went in the backroom and the other guy just checked my I.D. for like 15 minutes.

I've never been arrested or wanted by anyone for anything. So, I couldn't understand why it was taking so long. After what seemed like forever, the guy in the back room came out with a dog, and they all three went out to my truck. They walked around my truck with the dog looking under it and sniffing everything.

Then they got a mirror looking thing, on a telescoping handle and walked around my truck again. Then they opened the driver side door and one guy climbed inside. He was there for like 5 minutes, then climbed out and said something in French to the other guy. I thought they were finally finished and satisfied that I wasn't a drug smuggler or criminal.

So, just as I stood up to get a better look. The other guy and the (DOG!) Climbed up into my truck. I couldn't believe they just put their dog inside my house. The second guy and the DOG were in my truck for like 20 minutes. I thought I was in a dream (a nightmare) or something, I just couldn't believe they had a dog in my truck. After an eternity, they came back inside, talked for a few minutes in French. Then he handed me my paperwork and driver's license and said, "You can go".

I went out and climbed into my truck, I was so mad. They had flipped over my mattress and taken all the clothes out of my closet. They took all the stuff out of my little nightstand and even removed my pillowcase. The place looked like a tornado went through there. Papers and shoes and clothes were scattered everywhere. I was so mad and couldn't believe what had just happened. I still to this day can't believe they put that giant, smelly German Shepherd (mutt) in my bed. I was so mad and felt violated, but I didn't say anything. I was afraid they would throw me in jail if I got mad at them. So, I just left and headed north into Quebec.

Somehow, by the grace of God, I didn't end up in a Canadian jail that night. I didn't know they were going to search my truck; no one had warned me. I had a .22 pistol I always carried with me. There was a cover that came off the dash on the passenger side of the dashboard. It was a fuse box looking thing with a plastic cover on it. My .22 pistol was inside that cover. Somehow, by the grace of God that dog didn't find that gun. Or I would probably still be in a Canadian jail cell today.

I did not like Canada. Don't get me wrong it is beautiful. However, I was lost the whole time I was in Quebec, all the street signs were in French. I couldn't figure out where to go, or how to get there. I stopped at a little store to get some Gatorade and directions. The lady wouldn't even take my American money and didn't speak English.

I had to stop and sleep on the side of the road and wait until the next morning to get directions from my dispatcher on where to go with this load. Somehow, the next morning I found the GM plant and delivered my load. I picked up another load right there at the GM plant. I think I was in Montreal, but I am not 100% sure. Anyway, this new load was going to Detroit, Michigan.

Man was I happy when I saw I was going back to America. Canada is beautiful, and I even did see some wild moose while I was there, but you can have it, send me a postcard. I was lost and scared the whole time I was there, and those border guards violated me, I don't care what anybody says. I went to Canada three more times while I drove for PAM trucking. It's better over on the west side where they speak English, and the signs are in English, but I never really liked any of it, and never plan on going back. I plan to visit Alaska someday, but I will not be going through Canada. I will either fly over it or get on a ship and go around Canada. You can have it, No thank you.

Chapter 5
Just Glad to be Back on American Soil

I got that load at the GM plant in Montreal and headed for Detroit as fast as that truck would go. I covered half of Canada in record time. You can see the Ambassador Bridge from ten miles out. It's a huge bridge that goes across the corner of one of the great lakes, coming out of Canada. It's monstrous and they always have it lit up like a Christmas tree, with tons of lights, year-round so you can see it from ten, or even twenty miles away.

That's when you start getting excited because you know America is within sight. I had barely spent 24 hours in Canada, but I was already sick of it and glad to see American soil in front of me. You must pay a toll to come across the Ambassador Bridge. Then you have to park your truck and walk inside the border control office with your paperwork. Showing them what you are hauling and where you came from and where you are going with the load. I parked and went inside.

Unlike when I went (into) Canada in the middle of the night, and there was no one there but me. This was the middle of the day and there were at least ten other truck drivers there ahead of me. I thought, oh my God, this is going to take all day. To my surprise though, I was only in the border control office for about 5 minutes. They process trucks very quickly when coming (into) the U.S. From Canada. I guess they are not really concerned with what you may be bringing into the U.S. They never walked around my truck, they never looked inside my truck. They certainly never put any (DOG), in my truck.

In fact, to my surprise, they never even came outside of their office and did anything. They just stamped my paperwork and said, "You're good to go". The whole thing took like five minutes. I guess we don't care what is coming into our country here in America. It seemed funny to me, to be crossing an international border between the two countries, and no one even came out and looked in my truck. I could have been hauling anything in that 53-foot trailer, and no one would have ever known the difference.

I jumped in my truck and took off. I started looking for the GM plant on the north side of Detroit, it was easy to find. Man, was I glad to be back in America. I had already heard movie stars and singers talk about 8-mile road in Detroit but before that day, I had never actually seen it or knew where it was at, it was pretty cool I thought. Like I said, life on the road in a Big Truck, is an adventure to say the least.

I dropped that load in Detroit and picked up my next load just west of Detroit in Lansing Michigan. This load was some kind of electric motors, and they were going to Mexico. We, however, had a drop yard in Laredo Texas for freight going into Mexico. So, I was off to Laredo Texas, which is just across the river from Mexico. It's just over 1600 miles from Lansing Michigan to Laredo Texas. You talk about a road trip and another adventure. Here we go!

Going south to Texas was a lot easier than going east to Pennsylvania. The farther south you go, the better the road conditions were. God knows I was ready to see some sunshine. I had seen enough snow in Pennsylvania and Canada to last me while. The job is a lot easier when the sun is shining, and the roads are dry. Plus going south to Texas meant I was going through Oklahoma and could stop and see my daughter Melissa.

If you read my first book, you already know I had a daughter who lived with her Grandparents in Oklahoma, after I divorced her mother. For the two years, I drove an over the road truck for PAM, every chance I got, I would stop in Oklahoma and spend some time with Melissa. I would drop my trailer in our Oklahoma City yard and go pick up Melissa. We would go to eat or go to a movie or go work out at the gym. I tried to stop and see her every chance I got because she was growing up so fast.

So, on that trip from Lansing to Laredo, I stopped and spent a couple of hours with her. I told her about all my new adventures driving a big truck. I really missed seeing her every day and watching her grow up. I wish I could have been there in case she needed me, but I knew she was okay at her Grandparent's house, they were good people.

I felt like I had a job to do and needed to be doing it. I tried to send her money every week while I was out on the road. I wish I could have taken her with me, but the company wouldn't allow it, insurance reasons, I guess. I begged my dispatcher to let me take her, even just for one trip. I told him how lonely it was out on the road, but he just said it was company policy, no passengers were allowed.

Being on general freight made it hard to get a day off. Those guys on dedicated runs have days off built into their schedule, but on general freight, there is always another load to deliver. So, every time I drove through Oklahoma City, I would take at least a couple of hours off and spend some time with Melissa. I could drop my trailer in the PAM yard in Oklahoma City. Then bobtail up to Melissa's house and pick her up. We usually just went to dinner or something because I didn't have a lot of time. She really enjoyed getting to ride around in a Big Truck though, and it sure was nice to see her. As I said, you really do get lonely out there...

Then I continued southward to Laredo Texas, which is about 650 miles south of Oklahoma City. It was a great trip and getting to stop in the middle and spend some time with Melissa just made it that much sweeter. I made it to Laredo and dropped my trailer in our drop yard. The next load that I picked up was right there in the drop yard. Our drop yard in Laredo Texas was full, with probably 100 loaded trailers sitting there waiting to be delivered up into the U.S. In the '90s we had the North American Free Trade Agreement, or (NAFTA) with Mexico and Canada, and a lot of (made in Mexico) freight came out of Laredo Texas into the U.S.

It was always easy to get your next load down there because there were always a lot of loads just waiting for a driver to take them north. My next load was a load of made in Mexico stuff going to the Walmart warehouse in

Oklahoma City, I was thinking cool, another chance to see Melissa. My dispatcher made the mistake of telling me that when I got to Oklahoma City, I could take a couple of days off. I was exhausted. I had just driven from Lansing Michigan to Laredo Texas in barely two days.

You see according to the Department of Transportation (D.O.T.) laws, a truck driver can only drive for ten hours straight. Then he must take an eight-hour break. The problem with this law is, you don't get paid unless the truck is rolling. So, to get around this law, I would use two logbooks. I could drive ten hours, then show my eight-hour break, and instead of sleeping just use the other logbook and keep right on driving.

So, when my dispatcher said I could take a couple of days off when I got back to Oklahoma City. I was already exhausted and should have gone to sleep, but instead, I drove straight through, right back to Oklahoma City. Which takes nine or ten hours in a big truck.

I don't recommend this to y'all drivers out there today, you could easily fall asleep and hurt someone. I had lots of secrets for staying awake while driving for twenty-four hours straight. First, (I didn't want to die!), and I knew in a collision at seventy miles an hour, with an 80,000-pound truck behind you. The odds of you surviving are very slim, (dang near anorexic). So that in itself is enough motivation to keep me awake. Plus, I did not want to hurt anyone else on the road.

Here are a few more secrets for you guys who may get sleepy out on the open road. First, you tend to want to go to sleep when you are all warm and cozy, so turn the air conditioning up to high. If it's cold outside, roll all the windows down, or crank the stereo up and sing out loud. Obviously drinking coffee or soda will help, caffeine right. All these things will help you stay awake.

Still my favorite is simply (chewing gum). You will never go to sleep while chewing gum. You must stop chewing, to fall asleep, so just keep chewing. If your mouth is moving, you will not go to sleep. Try it next time you need to drive all day or all night, it really works. I'm going to give you one more of my secrets, on how to stay awake and drive for twenty-four or even thirty-six hours straight, but you have to promise not to tell PAM trucking. I hope I invented this one in the mid-'90s and no other truck drivers are out there using it.

Again, (Do not Try This at Home!), even if you are a professional truck driver. Okay, Ready? Here we go. Remember when I told you about the first day, I got this new truck, and how it was a full-size sleeper, you can walk around in? Well, if you could go 1000 or even 1200 miles without having to stop for fuel, and you are only getting paid if the truck is rolling because you get paid by the mile. You only must stop about every twenty hours or so, to get fuel in the truck, right, and if you could pee in a bottle and just keep on rolling, and if you got enough food for the trip before you left. Then why would you ever stop! I'm one of those people who can't sleep if there is work to be done. So, I may as well just keep on driving, right?

Wrong, it is a bad idea and people get hurt or killed every day by other people who fell asleep at the wheel. Anyway, what I would do is this. Set the cruise control at seventy mph, or whatever the speed limit was, and I would get up and stretch my legs. I could stand beside the driver's seat and hold the steering wheel with one hand. I would bend and stretch and even sometimes do jumping jacks or squats. I even carried a twenty-five-pound dumbbell around in my truck. I would stand up, not in town, but out on the open road. When I did not see any other cars around me. I would do exercises and work out with that dumbbell, right in between the two front seats of that truck, doing seventy miles an hour down the highway.

Again, I don't recommend this to you guys out there today, it is extremely dangerous, even for seasoned professional drivers, but I had to do it that way. Have you ever tried setting in one spot for fifteen or twenty hours straight? At some point, you must stand up and stretch out. Somehow, by the grace of God, I have never been involved in an accident that was my fault, but I was young and dumb, I would never try that today, or recommend anyone else trying it. Ever.

Anyway, after dropping my trailer in the PAM yard in Oklahoma City, I took two days off. Which was very nice because I had been at work for two months straight, ever since I left to go to truck driving school in St. Louis. I spent some time with Melissa again and got some well-needed rest.

Then the Qualcomm woke me up early the next morning. To my surprise, my next load was a load of dog food, going from the Purina plant in Oklahoma City, right back to Laredo Texas. As I remember it, it took forever to get a load at the Purina plant, I sat there waiting for two hours. Finally, I got the load and headed south to Texas. It was a nice trip, I always liked being in the sunshine of Texas, after the horrible driving conditions in Pennsylvania and Canada.

By the way, dog food is like the opposite of hauling baby diapers. A 53-foot trailer loaded with dog food is one of the heaviest things you can legally haul. With a load of dog food, the truck is maxed out at 80,000 pounds. The truck and the driver must both work harder when the truck is maxed out in weight. It takes longer to get the truck up to speed, and it takes a lot more room to stop! So, when the truck is maxed out in weight you must be alert and on your toes at all times.

    I made it to Laredo without incident. Then about two miles from our drop yard, some guy in a little S-10 pickup pulled right out in front of me. Remember what I said? They will do anything not to end up behind that big truck. I had just taken off from a red light. The guy in the S-10 pickup was on my right-hand side. He tried to turn right and get in front of me. The problem was my light was green and I had just taken off. This means I was on the throttle hard and was grabbing gears to get up to speed when he pulled right out in front of me, and with a maxed-out truck that weighs 80,000 pounds. I couldn't stop on a dime, and I slammed into the side of his pickup.

When the cops came, I figured I was screwed because the guy in the S-10 spoke Spanish and the cops spoke Spanish, but I did not. It turned out good though, they could see by the accident that he was at fault. They gave the guy in the S-10 a ticket for failure to yield right of way, then they let us go.

I dropped that load of dog food at our PAM drop yard in Laredo Texas. I was glad to get rid of that heavy dog food load. I got my next load right there in the drop yard. I don't remember where that next load was going to. I remember those first seven or eight loads that I hauled for PAM trucking like it was yesterday, but after that they just all kind of ran together for the next two years.

I know I picked that next load up in the drop yard in Laredo Texas, and then the dispatcher made me come to the PAM yard in Arkansas. I had some slight damage to the right front fender and headlight of my truck, from the Mexican guy, in the S-10 pickup, that pulled out in front of me in Laredo. Dispatch wanted me to come to the main yard, so they could inspect the damage. It looked kind of like I had hit a deer. The front fenders and hood, on a big truck, are all made of fiberglass, and it cracks and chips pretty easily. My right headlight was damaged, and the fender had a big crack in it.

When I got to the PAM yard in Arkansas, I dropped my trailer and pulled my truck into the shop. I went inside to talk to my dispatcher, while the mechanics looked at my truck. Turned out, it was going to take several days to fix that truck. I loved that truck; it was practically still brand new. I think it only had ten, or twelve thousand miles on it. However, I didn't want to sit in the yard for days, or even possibly a week while they worked on it. So, I got into another truck. It was a Freightliner and looked just like the other one, but it was two or three years older and had a lot of miles on it. They sent me out west in that new, old truck. Where I got to see Flagstaff and Salt Lake City for the first time in my life. I also saw the Grand Canyon and the Hoover dam, on that trip.

That truck was a pretty good truck, but deep inside I knew it was really someone else's truck and I missed my other, new truck. It took me weeks to get used to this new truck, it shifted differently and drove different and just all around felt different. If you are a truck driver you know exactly what I mean. I got the job done though, I drove that truck for eight or nine months. I put close to 150,000 miles on it, driving it all over America.

Chapter 6
Go West Young Man

I think one of my favorite trips was when I went to California for the first time. I don't know if you guys have ever been to southern California or not, but if you haven't, you should go. It's beautiful, even in the middle of January. I picked up a load in Flagstaff and took it to San Diego, California, you talk about beautiful. The day I was in San Diego it was 68 degrees, and it was in January.

I made my delivery and headed north on Interstate five. The traffic is not bad north of San Diego, until you get up by Los Angeles. The drive up interstate five is right next to the beach and a beautiful drive, you talk about a different world. A few weeks earlier I had been driving through Pennsylvania and up into Canada, fighting the snow and terrible weather conditions the whole way.

This drive across southern California was an absolute thrill. I'm not sure I would ever want to live in California, there are too many people and way too much traffic, but I may go back and visit someday, the beaches are magnificent. My dad lived in Long Beach a few years before I was born. I wanted to go see Long Beach when I was in California, but I never got a chance. If I ever get to go back to California, I am going to visit Long Beach and maybe check out West Coast Choppers. If you read my other book, you know I am an avid motorcycle rider.

Anyway, my dispatcher dead headed me into L.A. to get a load that went back east into Colorado. I did not like Los Angeles, way too much traffic out there. I got lost trying to find my way around L.A. Thanks again to my trusty CB radio, I got some good directions from a fellow truck driver and then I quickly got the hell out of Los Angeles. Two days later I was over near Denver, making my next delivery. As you might imagine, the weather conditions are somewhat different around Denver in January, then they are in southern California, but what an adventure.

During my two years driving over the road for PAM trucking, I saw the Grand canyon, the Hoover dam, the Pacific ocean, the Atlantic ocean, the Gulf of Mexico, the Colorado mountains, half of Canada, the hills of Tennessee, the mountains of Pennsylvania, the Chicago skyline, the snow in Wisconsin, and the even more snow in Pennsylvania!, the hills of South Dakota, the rivers and mountains of Idaho, the snows of Wyoming, the swamps of Louisiana, the beauty that is Florida, the great lakes of Ohio, the cold weather and the great people of Maine, the battle ships of Virginia, The Great State of Texas!, the (peach) water tower in Georgia, the lights and traffic in New York, the truck stops in Arkansas ha-ha, the beaches of South Carolina, the awesome natural beauty of Vermont, the Colorado river, the Black Hills of South Dakota, the flat lands of Kansas, the Golden Gate bridge in San Francisco, the Ambassador bridge that goes from Detroit to Canada, The Mackinac Bridge in Northern

Michigan, (If you haven't seen the Mackinac Bridge, you should go see it, it is worth the trip, It is over five miles long and goes across two of the great lakes. What a magnificent sight to behold). Interstate 10 that is a bridge across Louisiana, the George Washington Bridge in NYC, the Appalachian Mountains of Tennessee, I have actually eaten Boston baked beans in Boston, had a Kansas City strip in Kansas city, had a Philadelphia cheesesteak in Philadelphia, had real Wisconsin cheese in Wisconsin, had a Chicago style pizza in Chicago, had real Mexican food in Mexico, had a San Francisco treat in San Francisco, had a peach in Georgia, eaten real Creole food in Louisiana, had potatoes in Idaho, got violated by Canadians in Canada :) , and so, so, so, so, so much more. What an adventure! What a job!

    I challenge you guys right now! If you are a young man like I was, and college did not work out, or the military did not work out. Or your whatever career has not worked out the way you planned. Or maybe you are like I was, and an accident has left you partially disabled, and you can no longer do manual labor like you used to. Or maybe you are just tired of what you are doing and it is time for a change. I challenge you to take a long look at over the road truck driving. It will give you a chance to see the entire country of America and make a good living while doing so. Plus, they are always short handed and looking for good drivers.

In the mid-'90s, I made $1000 a week, right out of driving school, and later made $1200 a week. All you must do is go through three or four weeks of truck driver training school. Then, after you graduate, the school will help you find your first trucking job. Then you are on the road getting paid to see the whole countryside, and you talk about the adventure of a lifetime. I promise you will love it out there, and I promise you will see and learn things you did not know about America. Go try it, I dare you!

After I slid my way across Colorado, I got a load going to Green Bay Wisconsin. If you read my other book, you know my dad lived in Wisconsin. My dad lived just north of Eau Claire

Wisconsin. So, I knew that going from Denver to Green Bay, I had a chance to stop and visit with my dad in Wisconsin. I was again hauling parts for General Motors and those GM loads are always pressed for time. We were told from day one, that we could never be late with a load for General Motors.

I was told that if a GM load was late and an assembly line was shut down while waiting on parts. General Motors would charge PAM trucking $10,000 an hour for the shutdown until the parts arrived, and the line was up and running again. So, you could not goof around when you were hauling parts for General Motors. You didn't even want to take a chance of being late. So, you had to hurry and make sure you would get there on time.

However, I knew I would make it on time, I had never been late yet, and I did not sit around like a lot of drivers do. I kept the left door closed and kept the truck rolling. As I said, I got paid by the mile and I couldn't make money unless the truck was rolling. I knew if I kept to my schedule, I could stop and see my dad for an hour or two in Wisconsin.

I called dad from Colorado before I took off and told him when and where to meet me. I met him at a truck stop outside of Eau Claire. We went and had lunch together. I told him about all my new adventures driving a big truck across the country. We talked about his mom, who was getting old, and about my daughter Melissa, who was growing up, it was a nice visit. What a job! Who knows when I would have made it to Wisconsin to see him if I had not been on the road in a big truck. Plus, this way, I got paid to drive to Wisconsin. What a job! ...

After I made that delivery in Green Bay, I got stuck on a dedicated run for three weeks. This was probably the worst, most boring three weeks of my entire over the road trucking career. There was a dedicated run that went from Janesville Wisconsin to Flint Michigan, running parts between the two General Motors plants in those two towns. I got stuck on that run for three weeks because they were short-handed, and I just happened to be in Wisconsin at the time. It is about 400 miles from Janesville Wisconsin to Flint Michigan.

I would go over and back, on the same day. The reason it takes you so long is that you must go down and through Chicago and around Lake Michigan, there is no straight shot. You just have to go down and around the lake and go through Chicago which takes forever because of all the traffic in Chicago. You can take the Skyline Highway that goes around the main part of downtown and miss a lot of the traffic, but the Skyline Highway is a toll road. As a driver for PAM trucking, I had to pay the tolls out of my pocket and save the receipts and get reimbursed later. The Skyline costs around $12, (back then), and if you are going over and back every day for three weeks, it adds up to a lot of money.

So, a lot of the time, based on what time of day it was, and how bad the traffic was, I would just go right through the middle of Chicago. Which I might add is a blast in a 75-foot-long truck. Especially in January, when the road conditions can be anywhere from completely dry, to a foot of snow on them. Anyway, I ran that route, under Lake Michigan, twice a day for three weeks. At the end of the three weeks, I was bored to tears with it, and I hoped I would never see Chicago, or Michigan ever again.

I don't know how those guys run the same route day after day after day. My hats off to those dedicated run guys, I could never do it. My favorite part of the job was getting to go somewhere new every load. If I had to run over the same roads every day, I would not have made it six months on the job. Kudos to you dedicated run guys.

After nearly a month stuck in Chicago, I finally got a load going back to Texas. We hauled a lot of freight to Mexico during the mid to late '90s, and my time with PAM trucking, I always loved going to Texas. Maybe because I was born in Texas, but probably because it usually meant I could stop in Oklahoma and see my daughter Melissa.

Every time I drove through Oklahoma I would stop and see Melissa. As y'all probably know, your kids grow up so fast and every minute you are away from them seems like a year. It seemed like she grew six inches every time I was gone for a month. I was always so happy when I got a load going through Oklahoma. I know how tough it is for all the drivers out there and all the time they must miss with their kids, while they are out on the road. They sacrifice so much to get the job done, and I know it is tough, I empathize.

One year at Christmas time I got stuck in upstate New York for 5 days over the Christmas break. I made a delivery in a small town just north of Albany and got stuck there for five days. Christmas fell on a Wednesday that year and everyone took a five-day weekend. Even my dispatcher was off for those five days, and the fill-in dispatcher that worked over the holiday weekend, tried, and tried and tried to find me a load so I could get out of there.

No one was open, no freight was moving. Everything was at a standstill until the following Monday, I was screwed. I was stuck in a little one-horse town. I was at one of our fuel stops. but it wasn't a real truck stop, with showers and restaurants. It was just a gas station with nothing more than cold sandwiches.

You talk about the worst Christmas ever! That is the only time in my life that I went five days without a shower. I wanted to be in Oklahoma with my daughter, or anywhere but there for Christmas, it was cold and miserable. I just sat in my truck and watched TV for five days. So yeah, I feel for those truckers out there away from their families, especially around the holidays.

So, the next time you get up on the highway and get behind a big truck, and you get all mad and bent out of shape because he is too big and moving too slow, and he's blocking your view of the mall, or wherever you are headed. Just remember, that poor guy is at work 24/7, he probably hasn't been home to see his wife and kids in weeks and weeks. Or even had a day off in a month, and he is just trying to do his job, and deliver the very stuff that you are in a (big fire) hurry to get to the mall and buy. So please, cut him a little slack and maybe the world would be a better place for all of us...

Chapter 7
Another New Truck

By the time I got back to the PAM yard in Arkansas, I had been on the job for almost nine months. I had been zigzagging across America, from sea to shining sea. My dispatcher had told me to come into the yard, he said he had a present for me. I always hated going into the main PAM yard in Arkansas because you had to clear about 5 different departments before you could leave and get back out on the road again.

The hardest department for me to clear was the LOG department. There was a tall, bony, black guy that ran the log department at PAM, and I called him (The Log Dog). He did not like me very much because like I said, I ran with two logbooks and I drove way farther than the law would allow you to, every day. He and I would go round and round. I would tell him that I was a safe driver, and I was going to do it my way until I got caught by DOT and fined. I told him, I wasn't lazy, and I could not sleep when there was work to be done. I said that is just the way I am made. He threatened me with his own fine, but he never gave me a fine, but I always just hated trying to clear that log dog's department, so I could get back out on the road.

Anyway, I went in to see what the surprise was from my dispatcher. He gave me a jacket with my name on the front of it, and (PAM safe driver) on the back of it. I guess after you have been on the job for six months without any accidents or incidents or tickets, you get a safe driver jacket with your name on the front of it. Plus, I got a three-cent a mile raise, I thought that was sweet, a new jacket and a pay raise, cool.

Then after all this good news, he gave me what sounded like BAD news. He said, "I need you to go clean your truck out". He said, "Go get all your stuff out of your truck and put it in one of the dog houses". The PAM yard had some little motel looking rooms, that we called dog houses. I was thinking, what the hell, after all that safe driver award crap are they now going to fire me? Then he said, "Yeah, go get all your stuff. You are spending the night here tonight. Then tomorrow morning you are getting a brand-new truck." Wow! What a relief. I thought he was fixing to fire me. Then he said, "I want to take you to lunch tomorrow before you leave the yard," I said, "Okay". Then I went and cleaned all my belongings out of that old truck.

The next morning, they showed me my new truck, it was a beautiful (brown or gold), Volvo. It was a walk around, full-size sleeper just like the Freightliner had been. 99 percent of all PAM trucks are white, with red letters. I don't know how many trucks PAM has on the road today. But Dave the trainer guy I rode around with at the beginning, told me back in the mid-'90s that PAM had over 800 trucks on the road, and almost all of them were white. Somehow, I just got a brand-new Volvo that was light brown, almost gold looking. (Just like the one on the cover of this book).

Man, that truck was beautiful, it had all the bells and whistles. From the new banana mirrors in the front to some cool running lights that went all the way around. It had a microwave, a TV, a small refrigerator, even a brand-new CB radio. In the old trucks, you had to bring your own CB radio and hook it up yourself. This was one sweet ride; it was a ten-speed with a splitter. Man, it was sharp.

I have been told that they make automatic trucks nowadays that you don't even need to shift the transmission. I guess they made automatics for girls to drive or (girly men) who don't know how to drive a stick shift or use a clutch. I'm sorry, I know some women can drive the hell out of a stick shift, but when I was in truck driving school, it was the girls that couldn't seem to understand how to shift a truck or figure out how to double-clutch.

Anyway, this truck was awesome, I wish I had taken a picture of it that first day. This truck had less than 25 miles on it, it was brand new. I'm not sure but I believe I had the only brown, (gold) truck in the whole PAM fleet. I drove that truck for the rest of the time I worked for PAM trucking. I think I put just over 250,000 miles on it.

I spent the entire morning clearing the five departments, so I could get back on the road. It took forever to clear the LOG department and the safety department, but eventually, I did, and I got released to hit the road. So, I went to see if my dispatcher was ready to take me to lunch. We went in his car where he drove me downtown to some little Mexican restaurant, it was a pretty good place to eat. When you are out on the road and stuck in your truck 24/7 you don't get to eat at a lot of good, set down type restaurants, because you are always in a hurry to eat and keep rolling. Anyway, we had a nice lunch, just chatting about everything from the (LOG DOG) to my beautiful new truck.

Then at the end of the meal, he said: "Listen, I have a question to ask you". He said, "My wife and I are thinking about buying our first big truck and leasing it out to PAM trucking". He said, "I've always wanted to own some trucks and I'm in a position now, financially, to buy my first truck".

Then he said, "I want (you) to drive it". He said, "You are the best driver I have ever dispatched for". He said, "I already crunched the numbers, you have been averaging just under 4200 miles a week since you have been driving for PAM trucking". He said, "We have several (teams), of drivers who do not average as many miles each week as you do". (Team) drivers are where there are two drivers in the same truck, they just take turns driving, while the other one sleeps.

He said, "You are one of the hardest working drivers I have ever seen, and I want (you) to drive my first truck". He said, "For the past three years I have been keeping notes on all my drivers". He said, "You are the safest driver, who drives the farthest, each week, and I want you to drive my first truck". He then said, "I can't be your dispatcher though, because it would be a conflict of interest, and PAM would never let me dispatch (my) truck". I was floored and flabbergasted at the same time, I just stared at him for what seemed like five minutes without saying anything.

I never expected anything like that, I just thought he wanted to have lunch and talk about my new truck or something. I told him, I would have to think about it. He had just given me a lot of information to digest all at once. I said I needed to think about it for a few days and then I would probably have a million questions for him.

I got into my brand-new truck and took off down the highway. I thought long and hard over the next week about what my dispatcher wanted me to do. I asked him lots of questions during that week. First, I did not know if I wanted to give up this brand-new truck I just got, that I loved. I still think I had the only brown (gold) truck in the fleet.

Second, I asked him, "Who would be my dispatcher"? You guys need to understand here, dispatching is probably 30 percent of over the road truck driving. Your dispatcher must be on his toes, he must always stay out ahead of you. He must see the future and keep you rolling. There is no way I can average 4200 miles a week, with a bad dispatcher, that does not think ahead of me and keep me rolling.

For instance, if I am going to drop a load in Dallas in two days, my dispatcher needs to be thinking two days ahead of me, so he already has a load waiting for me when I get to Dallas. Instead of me getting to Dallas and having to wait for hours or even days to get my next load. The dispatcher has complete control of keeping me rolling. Therefore, keeping me moving and not just sitting around waiting for my next load somewhere. He must always be thinking ahead of me and being on the ball, so to speak.

Remember when I said I spent five days just setting in upstate New York one year over the Christmas holiday? that was a very bad job of dispatching. I do not blame my dispatcher because he was on vacation that week. Someone should have been thinking ahead of me and knowing I would be dropping my load that day in upstate New York, because of the holiday weekend, dispatch should have been thinking 5 or 6 days ahead of me and had me a load ready so I would not have to just sit there for 5 days over the holiday weekend. It is all up to your dispatcher to keep you moving.

So, not only would I have to give up my brand-new truck and move to a different dispatcher, but here was the main problem, and the reason I eventually had to decline the offer. My dispatcher was a young man, probably in his late twenties, I knew he had a wife and a new baby at home. He was fixing to go into massive debt and buy a brand new $200,000 truck for (me) to drive.

He had already crunched the numbers and he knew if I drove 4200 miles a week, he would have no problem paying his truck payment and paying the insurance on the truck. and making himself some money, while paying me. I got to thinking, what if I got lazy one week? What if the weather got bad and I could not make 4200 for several weeks in a row? What if I hit a deer or got into an accident and the truck was broken down in the shop for two weeks? What if his house was on the line when he could not make the truck payment?

In the end, I had to tell him I could not take the job. I let him down easy and said I think I will just keep driving this brand-new Volvo, PAM just gave me. I wanted to take the job, it meant a big pay raise for me, but in the end, I did not want his future, or his family, riding on my shoulders. After I declined the job, we never talked about it again. I hope he got a good driver and bought that first truck. I hope today he has a whole fleet of trucks.

At the end of the day, I am glad I did not take that responsibility. I had enough on my mind out there on the road, with the weather and traffic conditions, and making sure I got my loads delivered on time and safely. I did not need the added responsibility of worrying about getting enough miles each week to make his truck payment. So, in the long run, I'm glad I did not take the job, but thanks for offering it, man. It made me feel good to know I was one of the top drivers...

Chapter 8
Hitchhiking With a CDL

There are about ten or twelve places across the country where PAM trucking has maintenance shops set up for drivers to get their trucks worked on or just scheduled maintenance done, like getting your oil changed or a flat tire fixed, or at least in the mid-'90s, there were. There are probably many more of them scattered across the country today. In the mid-'90s we had one or two in Texas and the main yard in Arkansas. One or two in Pennsylvania, one north of Chicago. One over by Detroit, and I believe two in California. One in Florida, and several others scattered around.

A couple of months after I got that brand new Volvo, I hit a deer late one night while driving across Tennessee. I was very tired and trying every trick I knew to stay awake. I had the air conditioner blowing ice cold and the stereo blasting rock and roll. I was chewing gum and drinking coffee by the gallon, just trying to stay awake, I was out in the middle of nowhere. There were no other vehicles in sight, in front or behind me.

When suddenly about four deer, (Donner, Blitzen, Rudolph, and Comet, - I think), jumped out of the woods and right onto the roadway, right in front of my truck. Somehow, I managed to dodge all of them but one. I hit him, (Comet, I think), right in the center of the hood of my truck. He bounced completely up on the top of my hood when I hit him. Then he rolled off the other side and took off running into the woods where he came from, it did not even seem to hurt him. Which is crazy because I probably hit him at 60 miles an hour.

I immediately pulled over to check out the damage to my truck. It did not do a massive amount of damage, but those truck hoods are nothing but fiberglass. It cracked a long crack down one side of my hood. I opened the hood and got my trusty duct-tape out, I taped both sides of the hood, inside and the outside. I locked the hood back down and put a bungee strap across it and hoped it would be okay until I could get to a maintenance shop.

I was headed south across Tennessee and making a delivery somewhere in Georgia the next day. I believed the closest maintenance shop was in Tallahassee Florida, and that was a long way away from me. There ended up being one in Atlanta Georgia, which was good for me because I do not think that hood would have made it to Tallahassee. I figured the tape would hold it for now, so I kept on driving.

By the time I got to Georgia the next morning, several small pieces of fiberglass had already fallen off my truck. The crack was getting longer and longer from the vibration, I guess. I was afraid the crack would go across the entire hood, and the hood would break into two pieces and fall completely off my truck.

When I got to Atlanta my dispatcher had me drop my trailer and take my truck straight to the maintenance shop. At the shop, the mechanic told me it was going to take two days to get a new hood for my truck. Mainly because it was brown instead of white like all the other PAM trucks were. He had several new white hoods, but no brown ones. So now what am I going to do for two days? The guys at the shop said I was welcome to just stay in my truck in their parking lot for two days while I waited on the new hood to arrive, but I don't think so. How boring would that be?

I had been seeing these giant flatbed trucks across Tennessee, hauling huge loads of freshly cut trees or logs. These so-called (stick haulers), are everywhere you look, across Tennessee, especially around the hills of Chattanooga. Which I knew was just to my north, and I had two days to kill! So, the real question was, how do I get to Chattanooga?

I started thinking, I wonder if you could hitchhike across the country, just using your CDL driver's license, as bait. Then I asked one of the mechanics at the maintenance shop to give me a ride to the nearest truck stop. I told them I was going to take a shower, and I would get a ride back later. Some guy volunteered and gave me a ride to the truck stop. I went into the truck stop and the driver's lounge.

I asked a guy if I could follow him out to his truck and use his CB radio. I told him I was trying to get to Chattanooga as soon as possible. I told him I was a truck driver just trying to get home to Chattanooga, to see my kids. I told him I wanted to use his CB and see if there were any trucks in the parking lot that were going that way and would give me a ride to Chattanooga. He said, "Sure, no problem, come on."

I followed him to his truck and borrowed his radio. I said, "Howdy drivers, I am a truck driver just trying to get home to Chattanooga to spend a couple of days with my kids". I said, "my truck is broken down in the shop here in Atlanta and I got a couple of days off". I said, "I have a class (A) CDL license and a current medical card in my pocket and I am willing to drive your truck to Chattanooga, while you get some sleep". Within a couple of seconds, about ten drivers came back and said, "Heck yeah! You can drive my truck to Chattanooga, come on!"

You see it was a sweet deal for them, they would get paid for every mile I drove, just as if they were driving the truck. It is like 120 miles from Atlanta to Chattanooga, and they could sleep, and get paid. I jumped into a J.B. Hunt driver's truck and drove it to Chattanooga Tennessee.

When I got to Chattanooga, I used the J.B. Hunt drivers CB radio. I announced over the air that I was a CDL truck driver looking for a job in the (stick hauling) business. I wondered if there were any drivers in the area that I could ride around with for the day and see how the business worked? A guy came back and said, "My name is Mike and I'm in this (stick hauler) setting over here by the fuel pumps". He said, "Come on, you can ride around with me today and keep me company", so I jumped into the passenger seat of Mike's truck and away we went.

Don't kid yourself y'all, those stick haulers have a very tough job. It is nothing like over the road truck driving! As an over the road truck driver, I spend 100% of my time on the pavement. Those (stick hauler), truck drivers must go up into the woods on homemade roads and nothing more than cow trails to get their loads of lumber. They play in the mud, on some of the worst roads I have ever seen, all day long.

Mike told me, the job is easy when your truck is loaded. You don't have to worry about getting stuck, because when the truck is loaded and heavy it pulls right through the mud, but when the truck is empty all the tires do is spin in the mud, and it is a constant battle to not get stuck in the mud. Plus, if you get stuck it is going to be like a two-hour wait to get a tow truck out there in the middle of nowhere.

Chattanooga is nothing but hill country y'all. Mike took me down some of the hilliest, winding, curviest, muddiest, slipperiest, roads I have ever seen in my life. Mike wore mud boots all day, I had on tennis shoes, and I did not get out of the truck very much at all that day. After Mike loaded his truck, he had to chain and tie down the whole load so nothing would fall off. I had never even thought about loading or unloading my own truck. Nearly all my loads were (drop and hook). This means you just drop your trailer and hook up to another one, 99 percent of the time, I never even seen my freight, just drop and hook and go.

Mike had a much harder job, he had to do a lot of the work himself. He was out in the mud and slop all day, driving down the worst road you can imagine. On my truck, I hardly ever got out of the truck, and in my world of truck driving, I had never seen a muddy road. It was two different worlds.

My hats off to those (stick hauler) guys out in Tennessee, they have a tough job, but Mike seemed to love the job, he was always smiling and laughing. It takes all kinds of people to make the world go around, I guess. I spent about ten hours that day riding around with Mike. He showed me where the mill was and taught me a few tricks about driving in the mud. Thanks, Mike for letting me ride with you that day. I got out of Mike's truck late that evening, back at the same truck stop I had gotten into his truck at. I showered and slept in a chair, in the driver's lounge that night at that same truck stop.

The next morning, I did the same thing all over again. I asked a fellow truck driver if I could use his CB radio. I told him I was a truck driver just trying to get back to Atlanta to see my kids. I announced over the air in Chattanooga, that I was a CDL driver trying to get home to Atlanta and see my kids. I said, "I have a CDL and a current medical card in my pocket. I said I can drive your truck to Atlanta while you get some sleep." Wouldn't you know it, about half a dozen trucks were headed towards Atlanta? I drove an owner-operator's truck back to Atlanta that morning while he slept in the bunk and got paid for the miles I drove.

    We didn't stop at the truck stop in Atlanta. He let me drive straight to the maintenance shop where my truck was parked. I hopped out and said, "Thanks for the ride buddy". He said, "Thank you for driving, and have fun with your kids". I was still laughing when I walked up and started talking with one of the mechanics at the maintenance shop. They said my hood was there and they just needed about two hours to finish installing it. I walked down the street and ate a subway sandwich, while I was waiting.

As I have been telling you guys all along. What an Adventure! What a Job! What a blast I was having! I quickly realized, with my CDL license in my pocket, I could hitchhike anywhere in America I wanted to go and never even walk one single mile…

I wish I had been thinking about that about a year earlier when I got out of that first (crazy trainers), truck in Ohio and started walking home to Oklahoma in the dark. I bet I could have hitchhiked to Oklahoma City for free, instead of riding the bus for two days and spending $150. Hindsight though, right?

Chapter 9 - HOTDOG

During my time driving a big truck across the country, I have been from Sandusky Ohio to Corpus Christi Texas, to Bangor Maine, to San Diego, California, to Charlotte, North Carolina, to Duluth Minnesota, to Montreal, Canada, to Nuevo Laredo Mexico, and just about everywhere in between. I've seen some of the most wondrous, beautiful sights America has to offer, but being out there on the open road you also see some of the worst sights. I saw horrible accidents almost every day. Rain or shine, there would be countless accidents in every city or town you drive through…

One day just before sunrise, I was headed east on Interstate 70, just east of Kansas City. I came upon the worst accident I have ever seen. Two semi-tractor trailers had hit each other head-on at 70 miles an hour. The driver headed west on I-70 had either fallen asleep or had a heart attack and died, with his cruise control set on seventy. He had crossed over the center median and hit an oncoming semi-truck head-on.

The CB radio was blowing up with chatter about the accident for ten miles before I got to the scene of the crash, traffic was backed up for a mile. As I got closer and closer, I could see debris scattered all down the highway for half a mile.

Most accidents, when you come upon them, they are fairly contained in one area, where the cars hit each other and then stopped. This one was like no other crash I had ever seen, because the driver had the cruise control set, and never hit the brakes or even tried to stop. The truck just kept on going after impact and did not stop for almost half a mile. The truck driver headed west had fallen asleep, or died with the cruise control set, and never even tried to stop. He crossed over the center median and hit another semi-truck head-on that was going east on Interstate 70.

The sun was just coming up that morning and I bet the sun was in the eyes of the driver headed east. Because it didn't look like he slowed down much either before impact. The two trucks must have been loaded and very heavy to do that kind of damage. As I said, there was debris scattered down the highway for a half a mile. Where the two trucks did not stop but tried to keep on going after impact.

As I crept by real slow because the traffic was barely moving. The only piece of either of those two trucks that I could recognize was one of the giant diesel engines was sitting in the inside lane, where I was going east. The engine was sitting there in the inside lane of the eastbound traffic, but it was facing west, as if it were going the wrong way down the highway. It was just sitting there with the transmission still attached to it, with no other truck parts anywhere around it.

As I drove by real slow, I could see the cooling fan was still turning. I don't know if the wind was turning that fan, or if the engine was still trying to run, it was the strangest thing I have ever seen. A giant diesel engine and transmission sitting in the middle of the highway. Facing the wrong direction and still turning, with the rest of the whole truck missing.

There was not another piece of either of those two trucks that was much bigger than a basketball, I did not see anything else that I recognized. You talk about an eerie scene, everything was demolished and destroyed in the wreck, and fire that ensued. Someone said a prayer over the CB radio as they announced there were (no survivors). The driver who fell asleep and crossed the median was dead. The other truck had a man and wife team in it, and they were both deceased also. A minivan that was behind the truck traveling east was also burnt almost unrecognizable. That was the worst wreck I have ever seen, even to this day...

Another time I was headed west on Interstate 80 in Pennsylvania. It was the middle of the day and dry as a bone outside. I came over a hill and there was a truck laying on its side, covering both lanes of traffic. It was one of those moving trucks, like a 26-foot box truck. It was lying on its right side, on a small bridge. It was wedged between the side rails of the bridge stretched across both lanes of traffic with the tires and wheels facing me. I slammed on the brakes and came to a screeching halt! I set my parking brake, threw on my flashers, and jumped out of my truck.

    I was the only other vehicle in sight, it must have just happened moments ago. There was only one person in the moving truck. I could see through the windshield, a guy in there moving around. I hollered at him and asked if he was, okay? He said, "Yeah, just a little shook up". I climbed up and opened the door and helped him get out. He was a little cut up but seemed okay to me. I asked him what happened? He said the truck started fishtailing and he lost control. The next thing he knew he was on his side, wedged in between those guard rails. He was lucky, in my opinion, to be up and walking around after that kind of accident. We used my CB radio to call for help. A couple of cop cars and an ambulance arrived at about the same time. They checked him out and said he was okay.

It took two (Big Hook) wreckers to get that truck out from being wedged in between those guard rails. A big hook wrecker is the giant semi-truck (tow trucks), you see out there towing big trucks. They just about ripped that moving truck in half, trying to get it out of there. I sat there for almost three hours that day waiting on them to clear the road. By the time I could move traffic was backed up behind me for miles. Just another day on the road....

This is the third and final crash (wreck) story. I could write a whole other book about the wrecks I've seen, while I was driving over the road. Even on beautiful sunny days, you see wrecks everywhere, but I don't like to dwell on the bad stuff.

So, another time I went across the George Washington Bridge into NYC to make a delivery. The GW Bridge in New York City is a toll bridge. In the mid-'90s, I believe it cost $27 to go across in a big truck. I have read that today it cost $20 an axle. A semi-tractor trailer has five axles, which means today it cost $100 to drive a big truck across the GW Bridge, that is crazy. In the '90s I had to pay for tolls in cash, out of my pocket. Then save the receipt and get reimbursed from PAM trucking later. Today I imagine most truck drivers have Pike passes, or some kind of account set up to pay the tolls with.

 Anyway, I went over the GW Bridge into NYC to make a delivery that day. I was hauling Glad Trash Bags. I believe the main Glad Bag Company is in California, but this was a trailer load of Glad Bags I had picked up in our PAM yard in Arkansas that I needed to deliver in New York City. I always tried to time going through a large city, where I could go through in the middle of the night and not have to deal with so much traffic. So, I had timed it to where I would cross the bridge around three a.m. and hopefully, get unloaded and out of town before rush hour hit.

 I came across the bridge and found the place where the Glad bags went. I had to block the street and wake some guy up, to let me in. He said, "You will have to pull around to the alley and back up to the dock and we will get you unloaded", I said, "Okay thank you". That sounded easy enough, so I got into my truck and drove around the block to the alley.

The problem was when I got around to the alley, there was a small car parked right in the way. He was blocking about half of the entrance to the alley. Even though it was 3:30 in the morning, there was still quite a bit of traffic in NYC. I threw on my flashers and blocked traffic, while I jumped out and tried to find the owner of the car, thinking he would move it. I checked a couple of stores and hollered down the sidewalk a few times with no luck.

Then I drove around the block and parked back in front of the place I was delivering to, again blocking traffic. I went in and told the guy there was a car blocking the alley and I could not get in. He called the police and told them about the situation. He told me to pull back around there, and the police should be there in a few minutes. I pulled back around in front of the alley and waited, again blocking traffic. I waited for about fifteen minutes. Then I decided to try and back my truck down in between the building and the car that was illegally parked. I had to block all four lanes to try this maneuver, but it did not work. There just wasn't enough room.

People were honking and yelling at me. It wasn't even four a.m. and I had already pissed off half of New York City. I could not back up and get back to my original position, because of all the traffic. So, I had to drive around the block again and park beside the illegally parked car with my flashers on again. In case y'all didn't know it? A lot of alleyways in old towns like New York, Boston and Chicago are one way in and one way out. You can't go in from the other end because they dead end, and they are very narrow. They were not made for modern day trucks, that are 75-feet long.

Finally, a meter maid looking cop showed up. He said, "You can get in there can't you"? I said, "I have been here for twenty minutes trying every maneuver I can think of, and it just won't fit". I said, "Can you find the owner of this car and get it moved"? He said, "I'll sure try. If I can't we will have to have it towed out of the way". He spent about fifteen minutes walking up and down the sidewalk trying to find the owner of the car. Then he had me try and back in again with him directing traffic. I said, "Just like I told you, it will not fit".

After about another twenty minutes of him directing traffic, I got back into position beside the illegally parked car again. Then I guess he called for backup because another cop car showed up. Then they called for a tow truck to come and impound the illegally parked car. I waited for at least another twenty minutes on the wrecker to come and move the car. Finally, the second cop on the scene came over and asked me if I could get my truck into that alley if I pushed that car out of the way with my truck. I said, "I'm not sure, but we can try". I said, "I have been sitting here for an hour and a half and we need to do something".

So, the two cops held up traffic while I got my truck back in position and tried to back down into the alley, hoping I could push the car out of my way. I backed across all four lanes of traffic and right up to the car that was illegally parked. Then I set my parking brake and hopped out to take a closer look, before starting to push the car. One of the officers walked back there with me. He said, "Hop in and come on back, I will guide you in". He said, "If you damage the guy's car it doesn't matter, we are going to impound it anyway and the idiot should not have parked there, to begin with".

So, I started backing up, trying to push the car with my rear bumper. The problem was the car was in (park) and up against the curb. It would not move. The cop just told me to 'come on back and run over the damn thing'. I think it was a Honda Accord or Toyota of some sort. Anyway, I drove right over the top of it and smashed it to pieces. I left two giant dually tire marks across the middle of the hood, with my rear trailer tires. After I smashed it, it looked like something out of a cartoon.

I backed around to the dock and the guy came out and said, "Let me get the forklift and I'll get you unloaded pretty quickly". After I docked the truck, I walked back to the end of the alley to take a look at that car I had just run over. Before I got there, the hood of that car was probably two and a half feet off the ground. After I ran over it, the hood was probably less than eight inches off the ground. I smashed the hell out of that little car. I walked around it a couple of times, laughing my butt off. Then just as I turned and started walking back up the alley. I saw a tow truck backing up to that smashed car...

Because of that illegally parked car, I did not get in and out of town in the middle of the night. By the time I got unloaded and back on the road, the sun was coming up. I had to fight New York City rush hour traffic back across the bridge.

Alright, that is enough crashing and wrecking stories. I guess my point is, just slow down out there. Maybe increase your following distance. Maybe leave a little earlier and allow yourself enough time to get there, so you don't have to be in a hurry all the time. Or maybe just be aware of your surroundings. Or drive more to the weather conditions or traffic conditions. Please just slow down and be safe out there.

Google says 1.3 million people died last year on American roadways. It says 3,300 people die each day in car accidents in America, and hundreds of thousands more are permanently disabled.

I guess what I am trying to say is, if we all just slow down a little, and increase our following distance, and be more aware of our surroundings. Maybe, just maybe, we could save a few lives next year. We all know someone who has been in a bad car wreck. I'm just saying, you could be next, so please slow down.

To put it in perspective, a hundred years ago, there were hardly any cars on the roads in America, most people still used horses to get around. Just as they had done for hundreds and thousands of years before that. Today there are millions and millions and millions of cars on the roads in America. Imagine where we will be a hundred years from now. With the population explosion, there are more and more drivers every day. So please, slow down and be careful out there on the great American roadways...

When I was born, my dad gave me the nickname (HOTDOG). My dad called me hotdog, the entire 42 years that I knew him, up until 2010 when he passed away. I have HOTDOG tattooed on my right calf. Every time I look at it, it reminds me of my dad. During my two years driving a big truck over the road, I used HOTDOG as my handle on the CB radio. If you happened to be out there on the open road during the mid-'90s, you may have even heard me on the CB radio.

Or you may have even stopped and helped me when I had a flat tire or a broken-down truck. Or you could have even been one of the many good guys who gave me directions when I was lost and couldn't find anything. Or you could have been one of the many drivers I just talked all night with, while on those long road trips, just trying to stay awake. Or just a guy I chatted with at a truck stop while eating dinner. Or in a rest area while we stretched our legs. Anyway, I just wanted to say a big THANKS! to all the truck drivers out there. In the '90s there was a brotherhood, a comradeship, between drivers.

Most truck drivers would give the shirt off their back to help another driver.

I do not know how it is today. With cell phones and the Internet, and social media, everywhere. Truck drivers might be zombied up to the Internet like everybody else these days, I don't know, but I hope the brotherhood is still in the job like it used to be. Otherwise, if you take the friendship, brotherhood, and camaraderie out of it, I wouldn't want to be out there. God bless you guys and stay safe, keep the rubber side down...

Hotdog

Chapter 10
As a Child

If you read my first book, you already know that when I was two years old, my parents got divorced. My dad took me and my sister in the middle of the night and (ran), because he didn't want my mom and her new boyfriend to have us. We then spent 11 years on the run. We lived in some 65 different towns, in 7 or 8 different states, during those 11 years of my life. My mom would hire Private Investigators to try and find us. Every time she got close, my dad would throw us in the car and leave.

Sometimes in the middle of the night, sometimes in the middle of the day. If he showed up at school in the middle of the day, I knew what was happening as soon as I saw him. We would leave everything we owned because he was afraid to go back to the house. We would just hit the road for another town or another State. He would drive all night until he felt safe.

Then we would start all over again in a new town. Some of my grade school years, I went to 6 or 8 different schools each year. It is very hard to make friends like that.

During those 11 years, my dad would work in places where we could hide. We lived in small towns or hole in the wall communities. He would work on a dairy farm or a ranch. He even worked on pig farms and chicken farms. One time we lived in Hobbs New Mexico, where he worked on a peach farm, and I think they paid him in peaches because we always had boxes and boxes of peaches. We made peach pies and cobblers and jams and ate peaches and cream until we were sick and tired of eating peaches. To this day, I would much rather have a plum, Thank you.

We spent a lot of those years hiding in Texas, the state I was born in. Texas is huge and easy to get lost in, especially if you know the good hiding places like my dad did. We also lived in Wyoming, Colorado, Oklahoma, Kansas, Arkansas, and New Mexico.

One of the greatest things about driving a truck over the road for two years was getting to revisit some of the places I remember from my childhood. One time I went to Casper Wyoming with a load of freight for Walmart. When I was about seven years old, we lived with a Baptist Preacher and his wife and kids, in Casper Wyoming. His name was John Branch and I called him (John the Baptist). He was an old friend of my dad's from back when my dad was in the Marine Corps before I was born.

John baptized me and my sister one Sunday morning at his church when I was nine years old. I had always been told that when you came up from being baptized, you were born again and were supposed to be a new person. All I remember after coming up from the water and opening my eyes was the 150 people in the congregation staring at me and how embarrassed I was.

Anyway, that day when I took that load of freight to Casper. I spent about an hour just driving around town and seeing things I remember from my childhood. Like the view of the mountains and all the huge snowdrifts piled up to the top of cars. Then I parked my truck and walked over to a Wiener schnitzel to get a chili dog for lunch that day. They do not have Wiener schnitzel in Oklahoma, and the last time I had one was when I was seven years old.

Another time I was driving through Wichita Falls Texas. I stopped and spent a couple of hours walking around and had lunch there that day, just because I was born in Wichita Falls Texas and had not been back since I was a kid. I just wanted to look around a little and visit the place where I was born.

Another time I stopped in Caddo Oklahoma. Where my dad had ran an auto parts store when I was about 7 or 8 years old. I walked down the main street and tried my best to find the store but found no store that I recognized. There wasn't an auto parts store anywhere in town. So, I walked into the police station and asked if there didn't use to be an auto parts store in this block. The guy behind the counter said, "Yeah, this used to be an auto parts store." He said, "They remodeled it and turned it into the new police station about five years ago. Why do you ask? " I said, "My dad worked here when I was a kid".

Then he took me into the back room just to prove it to me. He showed me the overhead garage door that was still in place, where my dad used to bring cars in and work on them. I did not recognize any of that building except that old garage door back around in the alley. I remembered helping my dad get cars in and out of that very tight doorway as a child. That brought back a lot of fond memories of my dad. I drove through that small town and saw everything there was to see in about 15 minutes. Then I went to the only restaurant in town and had lunch. A Dairy Queen where we used to eat Sunday lunches when I was a child living in Caddo Oklahoma, I believe it is still there today.

Another time I was driving through Kansas and thought I recognized a dairy farm we used to live on, where my dad worked. I didn't stop because there was nowhere to park a Big Truck and I didn't think I would recognize anyone working there anyway.

Several times I was driving through New Mexico and wanted to stop and look for that peach farm outside of Hobbs, I always thought I would recognize it easily, but I didn't know exactly where it was, and I never seemed to have time to stop and look. However, knowing my dad, I bet it is pretty well hidden out of sight. If I ever retire and get the kids raised. I would like to go back to New Mexico and have a look around. Maybe even get another box of peaches.

As I said, just one of the many great things about driving a Big Truck was getting to see some of the towns, (and states) I lived in as a child, and re-visiting some of my old memories, and of course, getting paid for every mile I was driving.

Another great thing about driving over the road is the freedom. There is (No One) telling you when to eat lunch, or when to go to the bathroom, or when to go to work, or when to stop for the day, or really when to do anything. There is no supervisor in your face telling you anything. As long as you get your load of freight there on time and safely, the company is Happy.

So about once a month I would park my truck in a strip mall parking lot and spend the entire day in the movie theater, just to get out of the truck for a while and enjoy some good movies. I saw a lot of great movies in the mid-'90s while I was out on the road in a big truck, some are still my favorite movies today. Like 'Shawshank Redemption' and 'Good Will Hunting', or the first 'Jurassic Park' movie, good stuff...

There ain't nothing like the freedom of the open road. The next time your boss gets in your face and tells you to keep your desk clean or your pencils sharpened, or that you can't take a piss break for another 15 minutes, just think about it. Imagine having the freedom to take a break in the middle of a workday and enjoy a good movie. Or take your lunch break at 10:30 a.m. or 2:30 p.m. without your boss telling you any different.

There are no other jobs with the freedom you will experience like driving a Big Truck, twenty years later and I still miss it. Every other job I ever had does not even come close to the freedom you feel out there on the open road. When you come back home you can drive all the (day cab) and local trucks you want to, but it will never fill the void or adventure of being in a Big Truck driving across the country...

Chapter 11
Alligator- Alligator

I had been out on the road in a big truck for about two weeks, the first time I saw an Alligator. You must understand, I was very young and naive, even into my mid to late twenties. I was one of those guys who never locked the doors of my truck unless I was going to sleep or getting out of the truck for something. If I was just driving on a normal day or parked somewhere eating my lunch or doing paperwork, my doors were not locked. Again, hindsight is twenty-twenty and nowadays I would suggest you guys always keep your doors locked, for your safety and protection.

One day I was headed south across Texas, I stopped at our fuel stop in Dallas to get fuel. I pulled up to the fuel island and filled up both of my fuel tanks. Then I went into the truck stop and got a cup of coffee. I don't know if you guys know it or not, but at most fuel stations if you fill your tank, they will give you a free cup of coffee.

Also, the way truck drivers take showers is, when you get fuel, most of the big truck stops will also give you a free shower ticket. If you have gone several days without a shower because you have not gotten fuel in days and haven't gotten a free shower ticket. You can always just get on the CB radio in any truck stop in America and ask for a shower ticket. Most truck drivers always have plenty of extra shower tickets and are more than glad to share one with you. Just FYI, even if you are not a truck driver, if you need a shower, you can go to the nearest truck stop and ask. You will probably find a free shower ticket if you didn't have a ticket. In the mid-'90s most truck stops were charging 7 or 8 dollars for a shower; I don't know what they charge today.

Anyway, that day I was in Dallas getting fuel. After I filled my tanks, I drove around behind the truck stop and parked in their parking lot to catch up on some paperwork. It was just before dark, and I had just been sitting there for a few minutes. When suddenly, a young girl, slings open the passenger door of my truck and climbs in and sets down in the passenger seat. She just started talking 90 miles an hour and I could not get a word in edgewise. At first glance, I just thought she was lost and had accidentally climbed into the wrong truck, but again, I was naive, and she was a professional, who had *(obviously)* done this many times before.

Before I could say anything, she had rattled off her whole spill. She said, hi, how are you? My name is candy. Where are you headed? What's your name? You want a date tonight? I got all dressed up just for you baby. Do you like my dress? I bet you're tired, has it been a long day? I can give you a message. Do you like my hair? What do you like to do for fun? Do you want a date?

She said all that without even taking a breath. Then I said, "What are you doing? Get out of my truck"! I said, "You cannot be in here, you are going to get me in trouble, Get Out!" She said, "Come on baby I know you are lonely and need a date". I said, "I certainly don't need a date from the likes of you, and I would never have sex with someone who sleeps with ten different men every day". I said, "With my luck, I would catch some weird disease that won't rub off and might even kill me". She said, "Oh baby don't worry, I'm clean, I went to the doctor last week and got checked out". I said, "No Thank you! Get Out of My Truck! before I call the police".

It took me a good twenty minutes to get her out of my truck. I never saw anyone as resilient as she was. I thought I was going to have to call the police to get her out. You should have seen her. She had on (white) thigh high, zip-up boots, and a leather mini shirt, with a little tank top and pigtails. She looked like she just came straight off the stage at your local strip club. Not that I would know, but I'm just saying. She looked completely out of place at a truck stop. Man, was I glad to finally get her out of my truck...

Another time I was in Kansas City. It's been my experience that you don't usually see (lot lizards) inside the truck stop. They are afraid they will get caught, so they usually stay outside and hide in the dark between the trucks or somewhere. Just waiting for an innocent bystander to walk by just before they pounce on their prey.

Again, me being naive though, I went into a Wendy's restaurant inside a truck stop in Kansas City and there was a cute young lady who waited on me. As you know, it gets lonely out there on the road, and I started flirting with her. We started talking and she sat down at my table. She said, "I get off work in about an hour and if you stick around, we could talk more after that." I said, "I'm a truck driver and my truck is parked out back in the parking lot". I told her I drove for PAM trucking and gave her my truck number.

About an hour later, she came out and knocked on the side of my truck, I opened the door and let her in. We spent about three hours talking and even watched a movie in my truck.

She seemed like a nice girl, and it was nice to have some company and someone to talk to for a while.

After the movie, I went back inside the truck stop and got a pizza and brought it back to the truck. After we shared the pizza, she said, "It's getting late and I have to work tomorrow". Then she said, "If you want to have sex it's $100". I was (*absolutely*) floored. She did not look like a lot-lizard. She did not dress like a lot-lizard. She did not act like a pushy, mouthy, forward, lot lizard. She just seemed like a normal girl, and I was completely floored when she asked for money for sex.

I told her, no thank you, and I said there had been a misunderstanding. I even apologized because I felt like I had done something wrong. I told her she should not be sleeping with truckers for money. I said, "You are going to get an STD and it might even kill you". She said she had kids at home and needed the money. I said, "That is no excuse, just get a second job or something." When she climbed out of my truck,

I felt sorry for her, but I felt like I had made a friend...

That was the only two times there was ever a (lot lizard) in my truck, but they are everywhere across America. They are in the truck stops, and the rest areas everywhere. They would wake me up just about every night, knocking on my door and trying to get in. I learned quickly to keep my doors locked at all times. Most of these girls are being trafficked by some bad guys. I would see a car pull into a truck stop parking lot, just about dark, all the time, and let two or three girls out. I've seen it all across America.

I believe most of these girls are trapped and either depend on the bad guy for drugs, or he is physically abusing her and making her have sex for money. I think the only way to stop it, is if truck drivers just stop paying girls for sex. You can go to any club in America and meet a nice girl. Or nowadays it is even easier, just get on-line and join a dating service. You do not have to pay a girl for sex, and if you guys would stop paying them, they would soon disappear, and not be lurking in every truck stop you go to…

ZZ-Top wrote a song about (lot lizards). It is called (Alley Gator). They talk about finding her in Texas and chasing her across Louisiana. They call her a green-eyed monster, who will eat you up. Most truck drivers call them, lot lizards. ZZ top called them, alley gators. I used to call them Alligators because they will eat up all your money. Either way, you are much better off if you keep your doors locked and just leave the Alligators alone.

Just north of Oklahoma City, there is a place that used to be a rest area on I-35. The state closed it several years ago after a lot-lizard got ran over one night trying to cross the highway and get to the rest area on the other side. About a year later they went in and turned it into a scale for big trucks to stop at and get weighed by the state. They took all the pick-nick tables out and the restrooms out and put in a scale for trucks.

I do not know how much money the state paid to turn that rest area into a scale house, but I bet the state of Oklahoma spent millions of dollars just to keep lot-lizards out of that rest area. Today it is not even open anymore, it's all barricaded up. It is just an empty lot on the side of the road, craziness. If you guys would just stop paying them, they would disappear from the American roadways... No More Alligators!

Chapter 12
There Ain't No Feelin, Like 18 Wheelin

It is an old saying, but it is true. There ain't no feelin, like 18 wheelin. When I was in truck driving school, I put a new spin on that old saying. As I said, when I got to truck driving school, several of the students had been there for months. The course was three and a half weeks long, but you could not flunk the course. If you had paid your money, (which was about $2500 when I was there in the mid-'90s), you could not fail the class. You just simply stayed there and kept practicing every day and re-taking the test, until you passed and got your CDL driver's license.

So, there were several students in my class who were there before I came, and still there when I left. There was this one lady in particular that had been there for over six months. She lived right there in the St. Louis area and just kept coming to class every day for months and months. After I finished taking my written and driving test and got my CDL. I stayed at the school for about an extra week, while I waited for the driving school to contact truck driving companies and find me a job.

During that week, the instructors put me with that lady who had been there forever. To see if I could teach her how to back the truck up without running over every orange cone on the obstacle course. I tried every day, I would stand on the driver's side steps of the truck and tell her to turn right or turn left, while she backed the truck through the obstacle course. She would do great, as long as I was on the truck telling her where and when to turn. Then as soon as I stepped off the truck, she would start running over cones again.

She was one of those people who don't understand when the truck is going backward, everything works in reverse. She would turn right when she should have turned left and turn left when she should have turned right. She would run over every orange cone on the obstacle course, time and time again. So, the last day I was there, I put a big sign on the back of her shirt. It said, 'There Ain't No Feelin, Like Cone Killin.' Everybody got a big laugh out of it, but I'm telling you, some people should not be allowed to get a CDL license. Some people just cannot handle driving a Big Rig. I hope that lady never got a CDL driver's license, but I bet she did...

The contract I had with PAM trucking said I had to work for them for two years. The agreement was that they would pay the $2500 to the truck driving school I went to if I drove for them for two years. I loved the job, don't get me wrong, but at the end of the two years, I was not sure I wanted to sign another two-year contract. I guess really, I felt like I had seen the world, and I was tired of being gone from home all the time. So, I decided to park the truck and go home.

Here's the problem though. When you decide to quit, you can't just get out of the truck and go home. If you leave the truck somewhere other than a designated PAM yard, it is considered abandonment. If you quit and leave the truck anywhere other than a designated PAM yard, it goes into your permanent file, that you abandoned the truck. If you abandon a truck, you will never get a truck driving job again, because no one wants you in their truck if you have a history of abandoning trucks. So, to be sure and cover yourself you must leave the truck in the appropriate yard when you quit.

In other words, you can't just deliver your last load of freight to Casper Wyoming and get out of the truck and go home, just because you live in Casper Wyoming, and you quit. This would be considered abandoning the truck because there is no PAM yard in Casper Wyoming. Then someone from PAM would have to go to Casper and get the truck, where you left it.

So, it would go into your permanent file, that when you quit, you abandoned the truck, and you will probably never drive a truck again as long as you live. Y'all see what I'm saying, it works the same way with the trailer. You are responsible for the trailer, and the freight in it, as well as the truck itself. If you abandon any of these, you will probably never be able to get a job in the trucking industry again.

Here is the problem I had, the day my two-year contract was up, I was in Iowa, with a load on my truck that was going somewhere in Illinois. I did not want to sign another contract and keep working, I was finished and just wanted to go home. I had already made up my mind to park the truck and go home. I was not sure what to do. I didn't want the load I was hauling to be late getting to Illinois, but I didn't want to drive to Illinois either.

My dispatcher worked it out, just like he always had. Remember I told you guys' dispatching is half of the job. Your dispatcher must be on his toes and stay ahead of you. He had me pull over in Des Moines Iowa, and meet another PAM truck at a truck stop, and switch trailers and paperwork with him. His load was going to Texarkana Texas. This way I could go straight to the main PAM yard in Arkansas and park my truck. Then another truck could make that delivery to Texarkana.

My old Chevy Blazer was in the bullpen at the main PAM yard anyway. When I got to the yard in Arkansas, I cleaned out my truck and went inside and shook hands with my dispatcher. He said, "Good job, man! Come back anytime, we will miss you". I collected my final pay, and I fired that old Blazer up and drove straight to Beaver Lake, in Arkansas, where I fished and camped out for three days. Then I drove that old Blazer back to Oklahoma City. I could not believe that old beater made the trip. What an adventure though! but I was glad to be home.

  I spent the next three weeks looking for a driving job close to home, so I could go home every night. I filled out lots of applications but didn't have much luck. Then I started thinking, I wasn't sure I could go back to punching a clock for a living. I wasn't sure I could set around some job sight all day, being bored to death, looking at the same scenery, day after day after day.

  I had just spent the last two years on the road, going somewhere new and exciting every day. With no one telling me what to do, or when to do it. I had eaten lunch whenever I wanted to, for two years, not at noon, like everybody else does. I went to sleep and woke up when I wanted to, not whenever someone else said it was time to go to work. I only had one job out on the road. Get the freight there on time, and safely. The rest of the time you can do whatever you want to. There is no boss around, telling you what to do. I had gotten used to the (FREEDOM), of the open road, and now I wasn't sure I could go back to punching a clock for a living. Like I said earlier, There Ain't no Feelin Like 18 Wheelin…

After about three weeks off, I decided to try and find another over the road trucking job. I filled out some applications and got accepted at USA Trucks. The next day I drove to their yard in Van Buren Arkansas, for a three-day orientation. After the three-day orientation, they gave me my truck. The truck was an old Mack Truck, it was made in the 1970s. It had a million miles on it, and nothing seemed to work right.

That first morning they had to have a mechanic come out and give me a jump start.

The driver's window would not go down and the driver's seat wouldn't even adjust to fit me. What a hunk of junk. It was a cab over with a tiny little sleeper, you could not stand up inside this truck. You had to climb up into the driver's seat, then crawl back into the sleeper. It was a small one-person sleeper, I called it a (baby bed). It did not have a closet or any storage for your clothes. It did not have a TV, a microwave, a nightstand, a refrigerator, or anything else that brand new Volvo I had been driving for PAM, (had).

I think being the newest driver at USA trucks, I got the oldest, leftover, piece of crap truck they had, what a hunk of junk. I had been out of my truck at PAM for almost a month. I missed the job and being out there on the open road. I guess I was willing to drive anything, just to get back out there, and get back to work.

This old Mack truck was hard to drive too. It was not a ten-speed with a splitter like the new trucks I had been driving for PAM. It was a twelve speed with hi and low, and it had two different shifter sticks, sticking up out of the floor. One stick for the low gears and another stick for the high gears. I hated it, and never got comfortable shifting it. I drove it to Little Rock Arkansas and picked up a load for Dollar General Stores that went to Bangor Maine. Two days later, I was in Bangor Maine.

That old truck barely made the trip, rattling and hissing and popping the entire way. I thought it was going to fall completely apart, more than once. After I got unloaded in Bangor Maine, they sent me to Boston, to pick up a load going to Texas. I got that load and headed south. I asked my dispatcher if I could stop by the USA Trucks yard in Van Buren Arkansas on my way through, going to Texas.

He asked me, (Why)? I said, "Because I left my clothes bag in my old Blazer there in the USA truck yard". He said, "Sure, go ahead and stop by on your way through and get your clothes". Two days later when I got back to the USA Trucks yard in Arkansas. I went inside and handed my truck keys to my dispatcher. I said, "Have a nice life man and thanks for the opportunity, but that old truck is not for me". Then I turned around and walked away. I was only at USA Trucks for seven days, including orientation.

I could not drive that old beat-up truck, after getting spoiled at PAM trucking, driving their brand-new trucks. I got in that old Blazer and drove back to Oklahoma City. That was the end of my over the road truck driving career. It's been a little over twenty years since I was out there on the open road, and I still miss it. I think once you have been out there and it's in your blood, you never forget, and you will always want to go back someday, for as long as you live. There Ain't No Feelin, Like 18 Wheelin! :)

Chapter 13
Back Home

    I came back to Oklahoma City, where it took me a long time to finally find a job punching the clock. I spent the last part of the '90s driving a local flatbed truck hauling new steel. I made steel deliveries every day, to local welding shops and oil field yards, it was a pretty good job, I did it for almost four years. The pay was okay, and I got to be home every evening. So, I was able to see my daughter Melissa a lot more often. I had missed birthdays and Christmases with her while I was out on the road. So it was nice to see her more often and be here in case she needed anything. As y'all know, they grow up so fast. She is almost 30 years old today, it is hard to believe. It seems like she was just a baby yesterday…

    After I drove a steel delivery truck for four years. I decided to try some security guard work. It's pretty tough to find a job when you are 55% disabled in your back and cannot do manual labor, it limits your possibilities. I went to work at a retirement community, as a night watchman for about six months. Then one day my supervisor called me into his office. He said the center here is thinking about having daytime security guards in the future, and they have decided they want you to be the first-ever, daytime security guard here.

So, I said okay, and I was the first daytime security guard they ever had. This place was huge, we had a three-story apartment complex with over 400 apartments. Then in the back, we had duplexes for the real rich residents. Then there was a three-story nursing home in the back, with a full-time nursing staff. I think you had to be over 60 years old to get into this place. Then you would just spend the rest of your life, living there. I worked daytime security there for about a year and a half. As soon as they found out I had a CDL license with a passenger endorsement. They also let me get some overtime, as a fill-in bus driver. It was a pretty good gig, for an old truck driver. I liked working there, and the old people were some of the nicest people you ever met.

A few years later I bought a tow truck and I have been self-employed for the past 15 years now, I just drive my tow truck every day. I am about to turn 50 now and I do not get in any hurry anymore and no one tells me what to do or when to do it. Another pretty good gig for an old truck driver I would say.

Somewhere along the way I got remarried and divorced again. Nowadays I am raising my two younger children on my own, after divorcing their mother and getting full custody of them. They are 11 and 15, Rose and Jacob, the loves of my life. The very reason I get out of bed each day and go to work. My purpose in life, my very reason for being. I love you guys.

They grow up so fast. I still remember the first time I realized that Jacob was growing up. We were in our favorite steak house, about to have a big juicy one, he was about nine years old. His whole life I had always cut his steak up for him. I was afraid he could not handle the knife. In reality, he probably could have handled the knife long before this day, but I am a very protective parent. Anyway, I reached over to cut up his steak. He looked right in my eyes, grabbed his knife, and said, "(NO Dad), I got this". I have never offered to cut his meat up since:)

I guess the purpose of this chapter is just to say how funny life is. Just when you have broken your back, and can not even walk, and you realize your college career is over, and everything looks bleak, and life has smashed all your hopes and dreams, and the future is uncertain, and the whole world seems to be against you, and you are all depressed, and down and out, and you do not know where to turn, or what to do next, and you think your life is over.

(DON'T GIVE UP!), Do not ever give up. Pick yourself up and dust yourself off and get right back in the game. Even if the path you have been on your entire life is now completely blocked. Look elsewhere! Think outside the box, there is always another path. It may even be a better path than the one you have been on, and maybe, it is the path God intended you to be on all along.

Ever since I was a teenager, I said I was going to write a book someday. I waited until I was 46 years old to start writing. I got a fortune cookie one day that said (Your life will be prosperous if you use your creativity). So, I started writing, and now I have written two books about my life and experiences. I also have an idea for a series of children's books that I am going to work on in the future. So never give up, and never stop dreaming. We are never too old to follow our dreams!

T. J.

Chapter 14
Just F.Y.I.

Have you ever thought about inventing something, and dreamed about how that invention would change the world? How it would change people's lives or make their lives better. While at the same time, making you and your family rich in the process. Or have you ever dreamed of someday walking into a store and seeing your invention on the shelf for sale, and imagined how proud you would be? Or maybe, you had dreamed of your entire life of becoming an inventor, and dreamed of the day when you finished patenting, prototyping, building, and producing your invention, and you could finally give it to the world. Have you ever laid awake at night thinking of things you could invent?

Well, I have, my entire life I have dreamed of being an inventor and inventing something great! Ever since I was a teenager, I have kept a journal of things I would like to invent someday.

When I was 19, shortly after my daughter Melissa was born, I thought of my first invention, and I wrote it down in a notebook, with a small description, and a crude drawing of it. It was a shade that went in the car window, beside her car seat. It would suction cup to the window, and you pulled it down just like the shades in your house. It would shade your baby from the sun. About ten years later I saw that exact shade in someone's car, then I later saw it for sale in stores. I told people I had invented that ten years ago, but no one believed me.

By the time I was 35, I had about a dozen things in my invention journal. I had drawings and write-ups and pictures of these dozen items. To remind me of them in case I ever got the money to invent one of them. I had everything from a new kind of trash can, to a new style of a ladle, and several motorcycle accessories. I've always been a big motorcycle rider. So, a lot of times when I'm thinking about an invention, it has to do with motorcycles.

For many, many years, I have slept with a notepad by my bedside. Sometimes in the middle of the night, I will wake up and write an idea down. Or write something down, that I am lying awake thinking about. One day, when I was about 35 years old, I was watching an infomercial about a set of dishes this lady was selling. At the end of the commercial, she said, if you bought this set of dishes, she would throw in her new ladle.

This new ladle was exactly what I had in my invention journal. I screamed at my then-wife and told her to come and look at the TV. I said, "That's my ladle"! She didn't believe me, so I went and got my journal and showed her. It was a ladle with holes on one side, for picking up big chunks, and solid on the other side, for picking up juice or soup. I had a picture of it in my journal. It looked exactly like my invention; I could not believe my eyes.

When I was about 42 years old, I decided it was about time for me to invent something and try and get a U.S. Patent on it. I had about $50,000 in savings, so I figured we could afford to take a chance and spend some money on this (invention) thing. I thought if I did not do it now,

I would never do it, and I didn't want to live the rest of my life regretting not having tried. I was very naive though, I had never invented anything or applied for a patent before, and I knew nothing about the process, or even where to get started.

One day I saw this commercial on TV about a place that helps people get a patent. I soon found out they had a local office not three miles from my house, so I called and made an appointment. The guy I met was named Rick. I went to Rick's office the next day, and we talked for about an hour about my idea. The first thing we did was sign a confidentiality letter, saying they would keep my idea secret.

Rick was an avid motorcycle rider, like me. He loved my idea from the very beginning. He said in the six or seven years he had worked at the invention place. He had seen thousands of ideas come across his desk, and he thought my idea was in the top two or three ideas, he had ever seen. Now that I look back, that was probably just a sales pitch that he gave to everyone who walked into his office, but he seemed genuinely excited about my invention idea. He even stood up and just stared at me for a few seconds when I first told him what it was and how it would work. His face lit up as he said, "That is so simple, yet so perfect of an idea". He said, "Everyone who rides a motorcycle will want this on their bike". He said, "I ride, and I would love to have it on my bike". He went on and on for five minutes about how it was one of the best ideas he had ever heard of.

    That day when I left Rick's office, I was flying high, I (*actually*) thought this might work. Rick said the first step was for me to give him $900, so they could do a product and patent search, to make sure my idea did not already exist. I went straight to the bank and got the $900 and took it to him. I had not signed a contract yet. This was just the initial search to make sure my product was not already in existence. About a week later, Rick called me and said, "Good news, we couldn't find your product anywhere". He said, "Come on down to my office and I will explain the whole process to you, and if you want, you can sign the contract and we will get started on getting you a U.S. Patent".

The next day in Rick's office we went over the contract. He told me they had helped over 10,000 people get a patent. He said his company had thousands of people making monthly payments to them, to pay off their contracts. He even said, they had people on fixed incomes, making monthly payments to them, so they could get a patent and get their ideas out there. He said it would cost me $16,800, and it would be a two-year contract.

He said the (invention helper company) would show and advertise my product to at least 130 companies and try and sell it to them. He said the (patent helper company), would make a three-minute commercial about my product and send it out to these 130 companies. He said that a three-minute commercial would play on a loop, in two different Trade Shows, during the summertime of my two-year contract. He said they would promote and advertise and try and sell my idea. He said also in my contract, that they would submit my invention to a Patent Attorney for a U.S. Patent, in my name. I was thinking (WOW!), my lifelong dream, my goal, my kid's future. This meant everything to me, just to have a U.S. Patent, in my name, I would be an actual Inventor, it all sounded so good. I was ecstatic, just jumping with JOY!... but I was naive.

I had already decided that whatever it cost, I was going to do it if there was any way I could. When he said it cost $16,800. That was a huge amount of money, for a tow truck driver, who is a single dad with two kids to raise. However, like I said, it was my lifelong dream to be an inventor and I had the money in the bank, and If I didn't do it, I knew I would always wonder, for the rest of my life if it would have worked or not.

So, I did not want to make monthly payments, like all those other people, so I went to the bank and got the money. I went back to Rick's office and handed him $16,800 in cash, and I signed a two-year contract. He said, "No one has ever paid in cash before". He said,

"Only one guy had ever even paid half down, most people put down ten percent and make monthly payments". I paid in cash. Again, when I left Ricks office that day, I was flying high. I thought I had just taken the first step to financial freedom and my kids having a brighter future, but again, I was naive.

    I am not going to say that the company I went to has an ex-heavyweight boxing champion as their spokesperson, but they might have. If I told you their name, they would probably sue me, and get the rest of my life's savings. Anyway, when I was in Rick's office signing the contract, he told me the story of George Foreman. He said, the last time George Foreman fought for the heavyweight championship, he got paid five million dollars. Fifteen rounds in a square circle with a guy who wants to kill you and is hitting you in the face as hard as he can, trying to knock you out. For this Foreman received five million dollars. The day George Foreman signed the contract to make the George Foreman grill, he was given a check for one hundred million dollars.

I had always admired George Foreman, for winning the heavyweight championship at age 45, the oldest man to ever win the heavyweight championship. I also admired him for all his charitable work and for being a man of God, but now I wanted to be like George Foreman, after hearing that story from Rick. I thought all my dreams were coming true, but again, I was naive.

Over the next two years, the invention helper company did exactly what their contract said they would do. They drew up some simple computer drawings of my idea, with a three-minute commercial talking about it, and sent it out to 130 companies. Now bear in mind, my idea was a motorcycle accessory. It is something you would put on a motorcycle. Or maybe a 4-wheeler, or a trike, or even on a snowmobile, or a jet ski, maybe.

The invention company sent my idea out to 25 or 30 companies at a time. Then they would send me a list of the companies they sent it to and told me to wait for a response. Then in a month or two, they would do it all over again.

They would send my idea out to 25 or 30 different companies. Then they would send me a list of said companies and told me to wait for a response to see if anyone was interested in my idea. They did this four or five times during the two-year contract until they reached the 130 or so companies, they were contracted to send it out to.

You should have seen this list of companies they were sending my (motorcycle accessory) idea to, it was a complete joke. They sent it out to places like Mary's flower shop, Paul's Automotive, and Jose's lawn service, and Frank's small engine repair, and Snider's grocery market, and Joe's mule barn, it made absolutely, (NO! Sense). So, I called Rick to complain. He said, "We are partnered with over 800 companies who have agreed to review new products, and these are the companies they have to send it to."

I said, "None of these companies are even in the motorcycle business"! I said, "There is no way you will ever sell my idea to these people". I said, "If you had a new idea on how to cook a chicken, you would not pitch it to a tire and wheel company, would you"? I said, "You would pitch it to Tyson chicken, duh"! He said, "Well, these are the companies we do business with, and that is all we can do".

What a joke, they were just wasting my time and money. They were never going to sell my idea to anyone. Looking back, I am not sure they ever intended to sell anything. I now think they make enough money, just helping people try and get a patent, and helping people get their ideas out there. They do not need to sell (anything) to stay in business. What I am saying is, they take your $16,800 plus the original $900 for the product search, and that's all they need to stay in business.

Then they do whatever little bittiest amount they have to in order to fulfill their contract with you. Then they just move on to the next person. They never really intended to sell anything to anybody. I think they make their millions on two or three good ideas, (like the GF grill), and now they just make a living selling the idea that you (might) have a good idea for a new product.

If you do your research, you will find that they only have three or four products that you have ever heard of, and even less that you have seen on TV, or in an Infomercial. They are in the business of selling you an idea, (that you may have a good idea for a new product). They did everything they were supposed to do, according to the contract. They sent my information to a patent attorney, they sent my idea to 130 companies, and they put it in two trade shows in Philadelphia. Or they say they did, how would I know? I live 2000 miles from Philadelphia. Then I had to pay the patent attorney another $600 for filing fees…

Shortly after I signed the contract, Rick told me I needed to be working on a prototype in the meantime. He told me I should find a good engineering firm and have them get started on building a prototype. I looked online and the nearest engineering firm I could find was in Austin Texas.

So, I made an appointment and went to Austin. This firm said they could build anything your mind could imagine. They said they had

(CNC) machinist, and (CAD) or computer-aided drawers and 3D printers. That could make anything you could imagine. Problem was, they charged $175 an hour to work on your project. I gave (Bruce) at the engineering firm, $1500 down and told him exactly what I wanted. I signed a contract with him and a confidentiality page. He said he could build my prototype in six months or less.

Over the next year and a half, I would give Bruce $8500, and he would give me every excuse in the book, why my prototype was not ready yet. First, it was his health, then it was, he could not get the right parts from some distributor. Then it was, he needed more money, he always needed more money! After three trips to Austin and $8500 out of my pocket, I finally had to give up on ever getting a prototype.

I asked my lawyer to investigate suing Bruce. She said he had covered himself well in the contract I signed, and I would get laughed out of court, but again, I was very naive... Another hard lesson learned for me. I never got anything from Bruce and his so-called engineering firm. Not even a (CAD) drawing of my idea.

This whole process took three years of my life and ended up costing me a little over $32,000 in total. Hard pill to swallow for a tow truck driver, who is a single dad with two kids and a mortgage.

When you get a U.S. Patent, it is patent pending for the first three years. They give you this patent-pending period to go out and market, advertise, and promote your product. All the time trying to get investors and companies to buy your new product. Then after three years of (patent pending), you and your patent attorney, go back to the judge to file for (full) patent status. The only way you can get full patent status is if you prove to the judge that you have investors and companies ready and willing to buy your product.

In other words, you can't just set on your butt during those first three years. You must be actively out there working this idea into a real product. Your best advertising tool is to get a real working prototype, that you can show people. If I had a real working prototype, I would be able to walk into any motorcycle shop, or dealership, or manufacturer and this thing would sell itself, but without a working prototype, you have nothing to show people. You know the old saying, (A picture is worth a thousand words)? Well, a working prototype (is worth a thousand pictures)! If I had a working prototype, on my bike, it would sell itself. Thanks, Bruce for scamming me!!

After three years when we were going to go back and file for (full) patent status. My patent attorney told me it would be a waste of my time and money because the judge would deny my patent. Since I had no proof of interest, and no investors lined up, and no buyers lined up, and no working prototype. The attorney was going to charge me another $2500 to file for a full patent. At this point, I had no choice but to abandon my U.S. Patent, abandoning my dreams of being an inventor, abandoning my kids' brighter future.

All I had to show for all my work for the past three years, was a giant hole in my bank account where my money used to be. I want you guys to understand, no matter how reputable of a business the company may seem, and no matter how many commercials they have on TV, and no matter how excited and sincere they may seem about your new ideas. These companies are only looking out for themselves. They are only trying to get (your) money into (their) pocket, and they will do or say anything to accomplish this. So please, be careful, and do not make the same mistakes I have made. Don't mortgage your kids' future or spend your life savings on a pipe dream.

Hindsight

If only I knew then what I know now. If I had it to do over again, I would just go pay a patent attorney $2500 to file for a patent for me. Then I would take all my money and build a prototype. Again, the prototype is your best tool, it will sell itself. Then I would take it around to motorcycle shops, motorcycle companies, and motorcycle shows, and I would meet the potential buyers in person and shake their hand. You know, the old-fashioned way. I would never go to a, (help you get an invention going), type place again. I do not care who their pitchman is!!

I guess you guys have seen these fidget spinners that are everywhere nowadays. The lady who first invented them was on the radio one day. She had made a prototype and taken it around for three years and pitched it to Mattel, and Toys r us, and all kinds of toymakers. She could not find anyone interested in backing it or investing in it.

So, at the end of her three years, (patent pending) period. She abandoned the patent, just as I did mine. Later someone picked up her patent and ran with it. She was nice on the radio and said she was just glad it was finally out in the world and people were enjoying playing with it, but I bet she was absolutely (dying) on the inside. I guarantee you if I see my idea on someone's motorcycle one day. I will probably pull over and rip it off and go shove it down Bruce's throat. :)

I am only writing this chapter because I do not want others to make the same mistakes I have made. So please think twice before you go to one of these (help you get an invention patented) places and spend your life's savings like I did. After a lot of research, I found that only about 2 or 3 out of every 10,000 new ideas make it big. So, the odds are probably better that you will win the lottery than you getting rich from your invention ideas.

I will probably work on it again someday. Maybe when I am old and retired and the kids are grown. I will just be much smarter and wiser the next time though because you can never give up on your dreams. Never!...

Dedication

I would like to dedicate this book to all the hard-working men and women, professional truck drivers in America. These people are willing to sacrifice so much to bring you all the things you take for granted every time you walk into a store and buy something. The old saying is, "If you bought it! A truck brought it!" I don't care if it is a sofa, a refrigerator, clothes or shoes, a new car, or even food and groceries. If you bought it in a store, a truck got it there. Period!

These drivers are some of the hardest working, dedicated, professional people you will ever meet. For them to get a class (A) CDL driver's license they have gone through countless hours of studying and testing and practice driving a big truck. They have taken hours and hours of defensive driver training classes. They are the top of the food chain when it comes to professional drivers.

I know they get a bad rap on TV and on the news. Mostly because they move slow and take up a lot of room on the highway, and I will agree there are a few bad ones out there, (just like in any other profession), that should not have even been allowed to get a CDL license in the first place. However, I am here to tell you, these people are dedicated, hardworking, professionals. Most of them have families at home, that they must be away from for weeks and even months at a time.

    To get the job done they miss birthdays, and holidays, and everything else with their kids. So, they can get the job done, and bring you everything you buy at the store. These people are more dedicated than any other profession I can think of. They are at work twenty-four seven, they live in their truck. Away from friends and family and children. All they do is sleep and wake up and go to work. Sleep and wake up and go to work. They do not have any other life. Life on the road is an adventure, but it is very lonely, and a very solitary lifestyle. Plus, the traffic conditions and weather conditions can be an absolute nightmare.

So, my hats off to all the professional, over the road truck drivers out there. I think you are doing a great job. Keep up the good work and be safe out there! God bless you all...

I would like to dedicate this book to my three children and two grandchildren. You guys are my inspiration for living and breathing every day. I love you with all my heart.

(Red Sovine - 'A Truck Driver's Prayer')

Dear God, above.
Bless this truck I drive,
and help me keep someone alive.
Be my mortal sight this day,
on streets where little children play.
Bless my helper fast asleep,
when the night is long and deep.
And keep my cargo safe and sound,
though the hours, big and round.
Make my judgment sound as steel,
be my hands upon the wheel.
Bless the traveler going past,
and teach him not to go so fast.
Give me strength for every trip,
so, I may care for what they ship.
And make me mindful every mile,
that life is just a little while.
Amen

When I was driving a truck back in the mid-'90s you would hear this poem playing on the CB radio just about every night around bedtime. I have heard it in cities all across America. The old school guys loved it. I hope it is still being played today.

As Paul Harvey would say, "And now you know, The Rest of the Story"

About the Author

    T. J. Wray spent two years on the road, driving a big truck, in the mid-'90s. He said he has seen the Atlantic Ocean, the Pacific Ocean, the Gulf of Mexico, and most of Canada. As well as everything in between. He said he has seen the Golden Gate Bridge in California, the Ambassador Bridge in Detroit, the George Washington Bridge in New York City, and everything in between. He said he has seen some of the greatest sites in America and met some of the greatest people America has to offer. He said, in his two years driving over the road, he logged over 450,000 miles, from sea to shining sea. He has a saying that goes, ("I've been from Maine to Spain, and I've seen everythang")... He says, if you get a chance, you should get out on the open road, and see all the wonders America has to offer. There is nothing like the adventure of 'The Great American Road Trip'!

The Golden Gate Bridge in San Francisco, California. Trust me when I tell you it is beautiful.

The Ambassador Bridge in Detroit, Michigan. You should see this thing lit up at night. You can see it from 20 miles away.

The Mackinaw, (or Mackinac), Bridge in Northern Michigan. This is the longest bridge I have ever seen. It is over five miles long.

The George Washington Bridge in New York City, another beautiful bridge. This is a double-decker bridge, with two roadways on top of each other.

If you enjoyed my story, please leave a quick review on Amazon or Goodreads. Your reviews help other readers decide what books they may want to read. It also lets the author know if they are writing something that people are enjoying. I love reading the reviews and feedback from my readers. So please take a moment and write a small review. Thank you and happy reading...TJ

Please check out my other books on Amazon and Goodreads.com
This is the second book in the (My Life) series.

The first book is (Our Teenage Years: Growing up in a Small Town in the '80s).

https://www.amazon.com/dp/B07KY6GFD4

Follow me, (or contact) me here for upcoming giveaway information and new book releases, or any other questions you may have.

My website
https://sites.google.com/view/tjwray/home

My Twitter page
https://twitter.com/TJamesWray

My Goodreads Author Page
https://www.goodreads.com/author/show/17726900.T_J_Wray

Thank you

Please check out my new book (The Adventures of CDL Mikey) released in Nov. 2019.
https://www.amazon.com/dp/B081727NZP
It's FREE with Kindle Unlimited and only 2.99 otherwise.

www.ingramcontent.com/pod-product-compliance
Lightning Source LLC
Chambersburg PA
CBHW070546010526
44118CB00012B/1246